of America

HOLLY

977.433

16

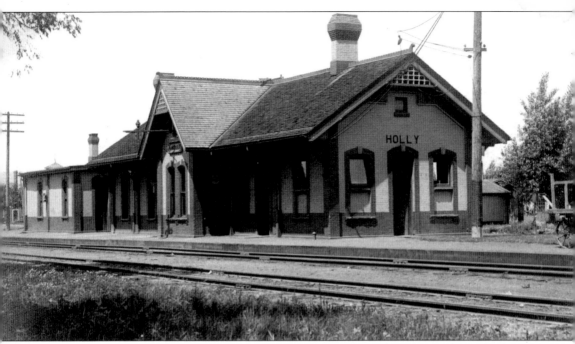

THE HOLLY TRAIN DEPOT. (Photo courtesy of James Hilty and Evelyn Raskin Hilty.)

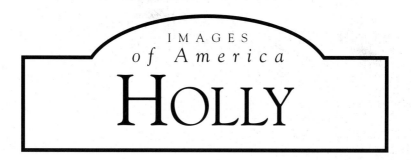

IMAGES
of America
HOLLY

Susanne J. Les and Greta Mackler

ARCADIA

Copyright ©2004 by Susanne J. Les and Greta Mackler
ISBN 0-7385-3343-2

Published by Arcadia Publishing
Charleston SC, Chicago, IL, Portsmouth NH, San Francisco, CA

Printed in Great Britain

Library of Congress Catalog Card Number: 2004110512

For all general information contact Arcadia Publishing at:
Telephone 843-853-2070
Fax 843-853-0044
E-mail sales@arcadiapublishing.com
For customer service and orders:
Toll-Free 1-888-313-2665

Visit us on the internet at http://www.arcadiapublishing.com

CONTENTS

ACKNOWLEDGMENTS

We gratefully acknowledge the great body of work left by professional and amateur photographers in the Holly area. This book would not have been possible without their effort, sometimes under trying conditions. Today, we all can enjoy their rich pictorial legacy.

This book was put together with photographs from the collection of the Holly Historical Society, unless otherwise noted in the captions. Over the years, the group of images has been sorted and the displays set up at the Hadley House Museum by industrious members of the society, most notably Gladys MacArthur and Linda Smith. The collection was not used in its entirety, as some of the photographs did not fit into the flow of the book. We tried to cover the development of our community for the first 100 years.

We also wish to thank Bruce Dryer, James Hilty and Evelyn Raskin Hilty, Don Simons, and David V. Tinder for sharing their photographic treasures with us, thus helping us tell the Holly story in pictures.

Thank you to Bill Whitmore for sharing his knowledge of railroad history. We also sincerely appreciate the ladies of the Holly Township Library, especially Shirley Roos and Margaret Rainey, for historical research assistance and for the donation of a copy of the *Centennial Anniversary Edition of the Holly Herald*, dated Thursday, June 30, 1938, to the Hadley House Museum. This incredible newspaper proved an invaluable resource. Up until now, there were only two local books on Holly. One is *A Business History of Holly, Michigan* by Vera Cook Husted, transcribed and indexed by the Holly Township Library Staff in the year 2000. The other book was . . . *And Then There Was Holly*, written and published by the Holly Oaks Middle School Pride of Patriotism group in 1976 as an ambitious school project. Some material was used from the *Holly Centennial Celebration Program Book* from July 2, 3, and 4, 1938.

The staff at Calvary United Methodist Church, the First Baptist Church, the Holly Presbyterian Church, and St. Rita Catholic Church, and Evelyn Lutz of the Seventh Day Adventist Church were very helpful on this project.

A special thank you to Tim Green for technical and emotional support.

INTRODUCTION

The *Holly Herald* newspaper, in its centennial edition of 1938, said that Holly Township was "23,040 acres nestled in the palm of the great mitten." There are three reasons for the development of this area: the Saginaw Trail provided access to the wilderness; the Shiawassee River was harnessed for waterpower; and two railroads formed a junction in the heart of the community.

Convenience dictated that the first settlement in the Holly area be located along the Saginaw Turnpike. These small sections of buildings were known as Stoney Run, located between the present-day cities of Groveland and Grand Blanc at Belford Road. The site of the first post office and school, the area was established in the 1830s.

Long before the first white men settled in the area, Holly Township was the home to many Native Americans, including the Ottawa tribe. In 1831, William and Sarah Gage moved to a cabin on the Shiawassee River. In 1833, their baby became the first pioneer child to be born here. Ira C. Alger was the first settler to live within what later became the corporate limits of Holly Village. In 1836, Alger built a log cabin in the area where Stiff's Mill Pond and Broad Street are today. At first the area was called Algerville, Busseyberg, and then Jonesville.

On March 5, 1838, Holly Township was organized out of the west half of Groveland Township. Jonathan T. Allen was the first supervisor. He had moved to the area from Howell, New Jersey. Allen had sentimentally named the township, and later the village, after Mt. Holly, New Jersey. The red berries of the local shrub called Michigan Holly probably inspired the title.

By 1843, Alger had dammed the Shiawassee River to provide power for his sawmill and gristmill. These were at the center of a small settlement which included a school. The village began to develop as a business link for the farming economy growing in the surrounding townships and as a marketing point for lumber and other products from the Saginaw Valley.

As the railroads brought growth and expansion to Michigan, Holly's importance as a trading center was enhanced and the small hamlet quickly increased in size. The first rails came in 1855 and the link to Flint was finished in 1864. This became known as the Holly-Flint Line, making Holly the first Michigan community with a railroad junction. By 1872, Holly's pathway out of the wilderness was completed, when a fourth and last line joined the others. The white pine forests of northern Michigan were being harvested and shipped to the East Coast of the United States along these rails.

The end of the Civil War marked the birthdate of Holly Village as an independent corporation. The years following were boom years for Holly. All goods and passengers traveling between Detroit and Flint by rail had to pass through the village. Between 100 and 120 trains would come through town during a 24-hour period. The population tripled between 1865 and 1870.

In February of 1877, the Ladies Library Association was started with a group of 75 people that met in private homes. For a year they met in the basement of the Presbyterian Church and then moved on to a building in the Balcony Block on Broad Street. The group started with 287 volumes and ended up with thousands within a few years.

A series of fires in the 1870s brought the first water works in Oakland County, Michigan. This was built next to the Mill Pond in 1880. The Holly Electric Company was also established in this area, in 1890, as it was water-powered. As the boom time for northern Michigan lumber decreased, other businesses took their place. The H.J. Heinz Company, Grinnell Brothers Piano Factory, and the Cyclone Fence Company were some of the larger companies that contributed to the local economy. By the turn of the century, Holly was considered second only to Pontiac as a thriving community in Michigan's Oakland County.

This area of the state is known for its 60 lakes and streams, all within a five-mile radius of the Holly Village center—once a liability for development, these waters now contribute greatly to the beauty of the community. Historic Holly is a nationally-acclaimed landmark, with 53 structures listed on the National Register of Historic Places.

One

EARLY HISTORY

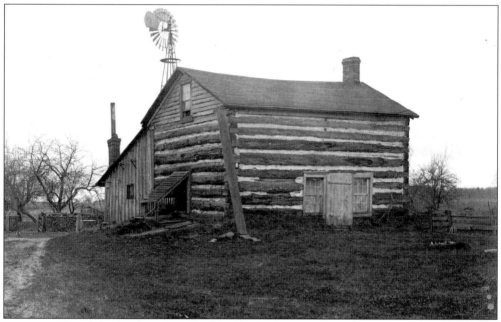

GEORGE WRIGHT'S FARM. This photo illustrates what a log cabin would have looked like during the mid-19th century. Sufficient trees were felled to supply logs for a cabin of about ten feet square in dimension. A fireplace of stone with a stack and mud-plastered chimney was built in the gable end. This provided heating and cooking capabilities.

The one-room first floor of the cabin generally had a six-foot ceiling clearance. This room served as a kitchen, dining, sitting, and sleeping room combined. If the family was large, there might be a sleeping loft overhead where pallets were spread out on the rough floor. A ladder and a trap door arrangement gave access to the loft.

The floors were generally constructed of split logs, flat side up. The roof consisted of a pole frame with overlapping split shakes to fend off the rain and snow. Gaps between adjoining logs were closed with soft clay inserts. (Photo courtesy of David V. Tinder.)

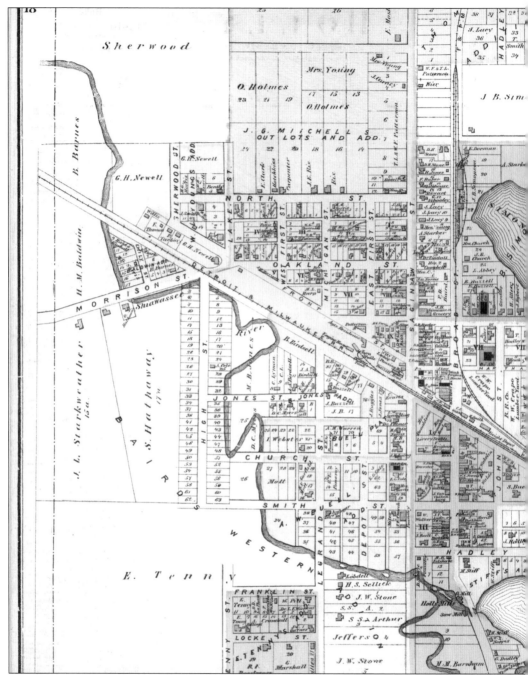

F.W. Beers & Company Map, 1872. This is a map of Holly Township from actual 1872 surveys and records of Oakland County, Michigan. One of the features that stands out is the railroad tracks that go both north and south, and northwest and southeast. Also evident are Stiff's Mill Pond, Simonson's Lake, and the areas devoted to farms. These water features are part of the Shiawassee River watershed that was important in the development of this area. The major north-south streets are Broad and Saginaw, intersected by Maple, Elm, and Sherman.

Listed in the business notices on the right side of the map are: Attorneys at Law Thomas L.

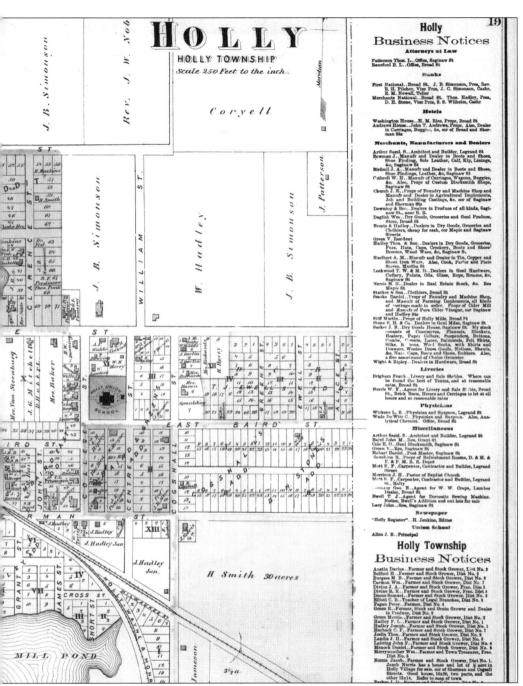

Patterson and B.L. Ransford; the First National Bank and Merchant's National Bank, both on Broad Street; the Washington House, a hotel on Broad Street, and the Andrews House, on Broad and Sherman; 30 merchants and manufacturers; two liveries; physicians Dr. Wickens and Dr. Wade; one newspaper, the *Holly Register*; and the Union School.

In a matter of approximately 34 years, the log cabin in the wilderness had given way to a prosperous community. The following collection of photographs illustrates the history of this development. (Image courtesy of Aprecis Group.)

11

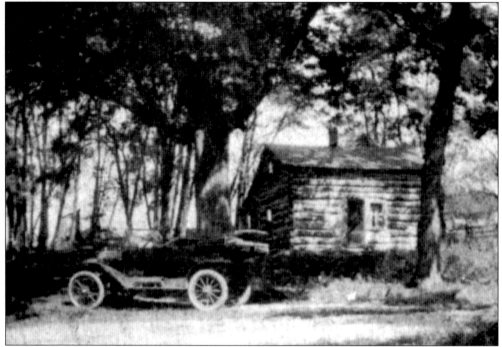

Henly Smith's Log Cabin. Henly Smith built this log cabin in the 1840s. Attached to the large tree is an iron chain, placed there so that the local Native Americans would have a place to hitch their ponies. "Michigan fever" was a common ailment suffered by many of the early settlers. An Indian chief gave a healing salve to Ira C. Alger to administer to the local residents. Numerous offers were later made to buy the remedy but Alger refused to sell. Ira became known as "Doc" because of his natural ability to cure people without a formal education.

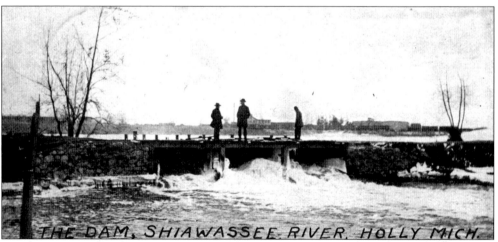

Old Mill Dam, Postmark 1907. Settlers were attracted to southern end of Holly because of the Shiawassee River. The earliest settlement, in what is now the village, dates back to the early 1820s with the arrival of Ira C. Alger. In 1843, Alger dammed the river where Holly and Rose Township border. This was a significant step for the little settlement. Mills were essential because they provided important services: grinding grain and processing lumber were most important during the frontier phase. (Photo courtesy of Don Simons.)

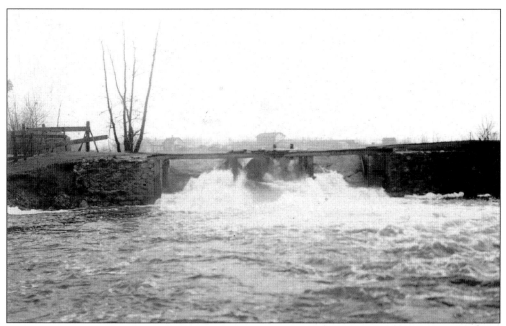

OLD MILL DAM, POSTMARK 1915. Ira Alger constructed a sawmill on the west side of the Mill Pond and later he erected a grinding mill, using water power with eight runs. The mills were sold to William F. Hadley who, in 1870, sold to William Stiff. Mr. Stiff installed a 35 horsepower steam engine and boiler. Railroad siding was laid south from the Grand Trunk tracks crossing Sherman and Hadley streets. Tracks also run along the north side of what is now called Stiff's Mill Pond, crossing South Broad Street, and along the north side of the Shiawassee River, west of the mill. (Photo courtesy of Don Simons.)

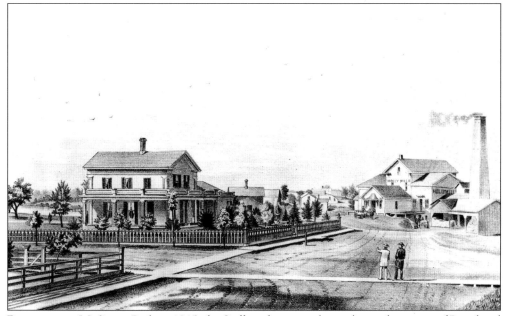

PROPERTY OF M. STIFF. Built in 1845, the Stiff residence was located near the corner of Broad and Hadley. In the background is Holly Mills. Later, the Stiff building became a well-known tavern.

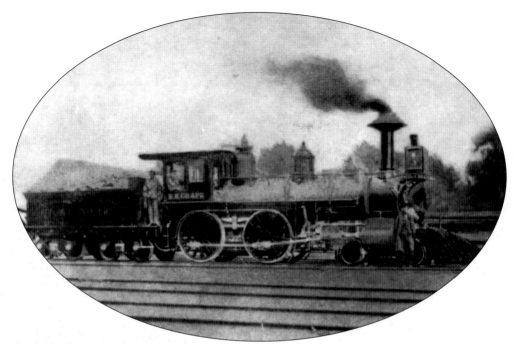

SKETCH OF STEAM ENGINE. This is an image of the steam engine, the first to run between Flint and Holly. Wood or coal supplied the necessary power for the steam locomotive. The Flint and Holly Railroad was built and owned by Henry H. Crapo and opened for business December 1, 1864. Because it was one rod wider than other streets, Broad Street became the right of way. Crapo was the first to use rolled steel construction on the rails in the United States. A year later, two trains ran on the track, carrying 400 passengers daily.

At the time, a brakeman had to sit in each car and when a signal was given from the engine, each brakeman had to apply the car's brakes. Among the brakemen, it was a mark of honor to have lost their fingers. Before couplers were perfected, the men used a link and pin system to connect cars together. The brakemen had to hold the couplers together with bare hands to link two cars.

Holly had a water tank, a turntable, and engine repair shops on the west side of Simonson Lake. The railroad was sold to the Pere Marquette in 1869. In 1876 the rail was extended to Monroe as the Holly, Wayne and Monroe Railroad. The railway followed the high ground between the lakes on old Indian trails. (Photo courtesy of James Hilty and Evelyn Raskin Hilty.)

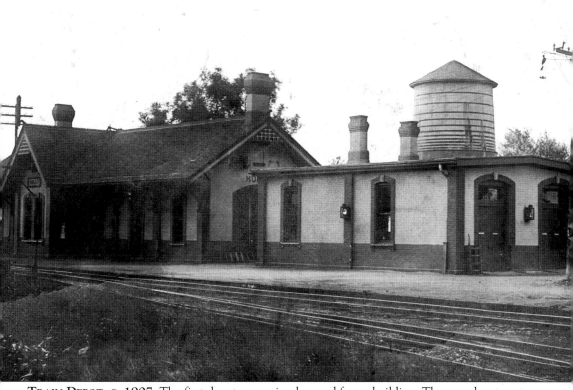

TRAIN DEPOT, C. 1907. The first depot was a simple wood frame building. The new depot was described in the following article excerpted from the February 18, 1886 edition of the *Holly Advertiser*: "The exterior body of the building was laid with pressed brick, all facing, projections and pilasters were of white brick, with cut stone water table, sills, caps, corbels, and key stones. This façade was surmounted by a wide wooden cornice painted dark brown and red, making a contrast pleasing to the eye. The interior walls were white brick painted and varnished making a good surface and affording no place for bugs or spiders. The ceiling cornices and all inside woodwork of waiting rooms and offices were of Norway pine finished in oils. The ticket offices were nearly in the center, each with handsome bay windows. An archway, seven feet wide, was between them connecting the waiting rooms. The ticket windows fitted with silver-plated bars opened into this passage. The new depot contained a telegraph office. This office housed eight telegraph lines, which belonged to the Western Union Company." (Photo courtesy of James Hilty and Evelyn Raskin Hilty.)

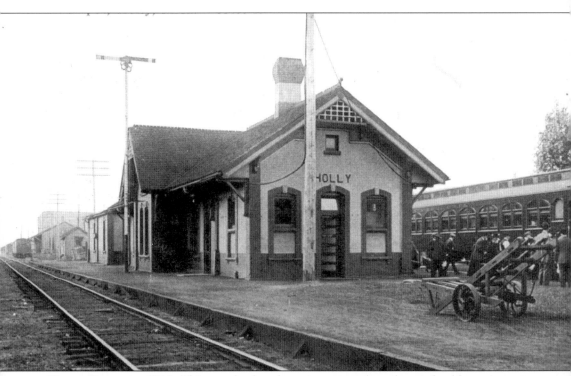

TRAIN DEPOT, C. 1915. This was the first depot in town to have hot and cold running water, electricity, and drinking fountains in combination. According to the *Holly Advertiser*, "west of the offices, in the general waiting room, was an outstanding lunch counter. It had a walnut counter with large windows both above and below that added to the general effect. The inside was fitted with drawers, cupboards, and a sink. The ladies [*sic*] waiting room was east of the main offices. There was a handsome fireplace with a dark marble mantle and furnishings and nickel rails gave a cozy, homelike appearance to the room. Opening from this room was the ladies [*sic*] lavatory, wash bowl, glass, etc. A Smith & Owen Heater stood in one corner." The present depot is the third one on this site. Since 2002, the Depot Restoration Committee has been restoring the depot to the original plan when it was built. (Photo courtesy of James Hilty and Evelyn Raskin Hilty.)

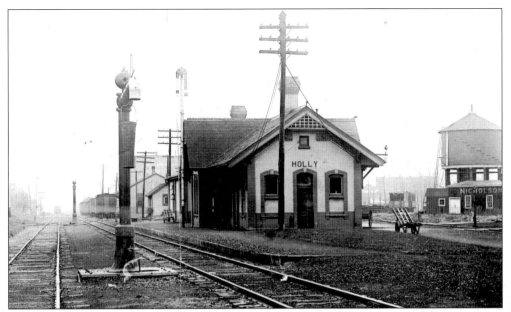

TRAIN DEPOT, C. 1913. Holly's previous growth was due largely to its location; it was a stagecoach junction first and then served the railroads. Its settlement was also due in part to the $2-an-acre land grants. Holly was located 17 miles from Flint, 22 miles from Pontiac, 39 miles from Ann Arbor, and 45 miles from Detroit, all major cities in Michigan.

Two water spouts, as shown in this photograph to the front and left of the station, were used to refill water tanks of the passenger train tenders that stopped in Holly. Also shown is the hard-packed stone passenger loading platform, which was usually made of wood. (Photo courtesy of James Hilty and Evelyn Raskin Hilty.)

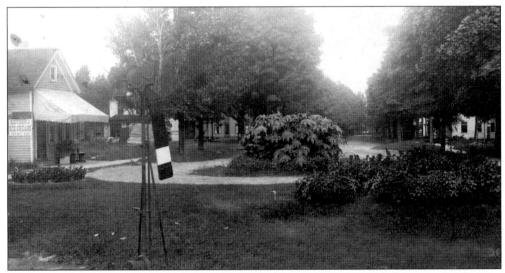

DEAD END ON WASHINGTON STREET. At the spot where Washington Street stopped at the railroad tracks, there was an area for hacks to deliver and pick up passengers. In the foreground is a switch stand, used to mark the position of another track. On the left side is a convenience store that served passengers getting off and on. Holly was usually a 10-minute stop. (Photo courtesy of James Hilty and Evelyn Raskin Hilty.)

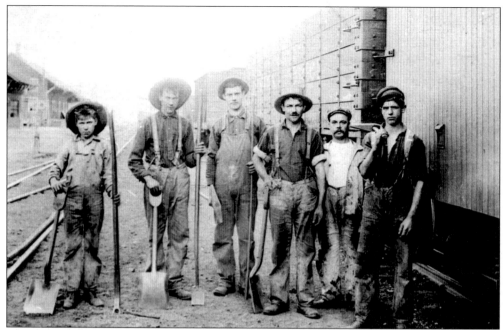

YOUNG MEN WORKING THE RAILROAD. This picture was taken before 1903 and shows young men ready for a day of dangerous manual labor maintaining the tracks. From left to right are Tom White, Jim White, unidentified, and John White. The other two are also unidentified. Tom White was killed when he was 18 years old.

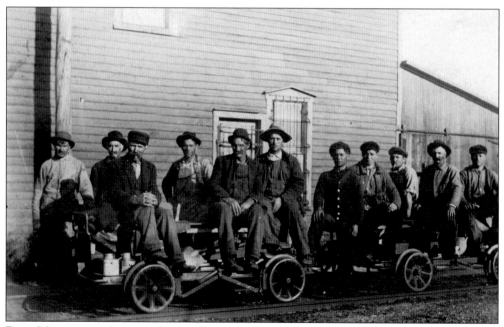

PERE MARQUETTE SECTION MEN. The section gang was responsible for maintaining tracks. Sitting on the speeders allowed them to go up and down the rails with their equipment to the repair sites. Sitting third from left is Louie Schwartz. The gang boss was Bedgdon Almond. The rest are unidentified. (Photo courtesy of Louise Forbes.)

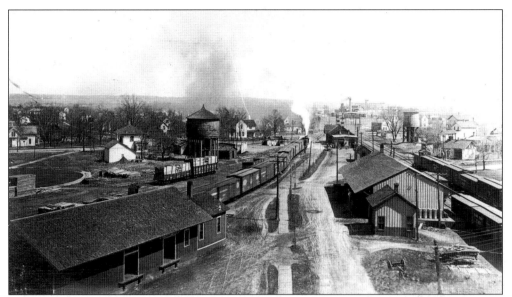

LOOKING EAST FROM OPERA HOUSE, UPPER STORY. This photo was taken around 1907 and shows the area looking east from the Opera House. On the right is the old freight depot completely separate from the main depot. On the left is the Pere Marquette freight depot near the water tower. In the winter, the water towers were generally heated by wood to keep the water from freezing. The train on the left center is departing Holly for Detroit. (Photo courtesy of James Hilty and Evelyn Raskin Hilty.)

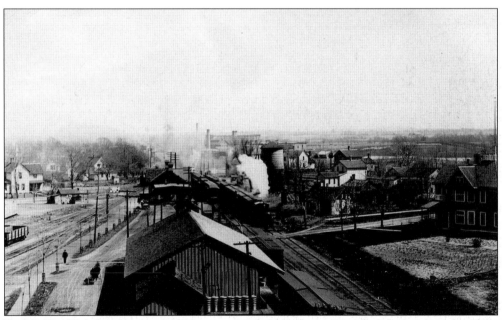

BIRD'S-EYE VIEW OF RAILROAD YARD, C. 1913. Looking east, in the left center, is the Holly Union Depot, serving two railroads. In the foreground is the Freight Depot for the Detroit, Grand Haven and Milwaukee Railroad. Note the ball field across the tracks, now the site of the Village Fire House. Visible is the sidewalk, which runs from the hotels on Broad Street to the train station. (Photo courtesy of David V. Tinder.)

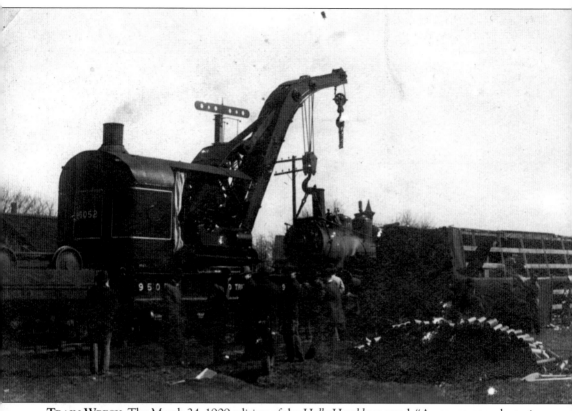

TRAIN WRECK. The March 24, 1909 edition of the *Holly Herald* reported: "A very spectacular train wreck happened on the Pere Marquette at about 8:45 Monday morning, when one of their biggest engines jumped the track on Martha Street curve and plowed through McLaughlin Brothers Elevator. The engine left the rails at the switch, just south of the crossing and pushed by the heavy train, ran along the ties for a few rods, and then turned almost at right angles, and entered the elevator at the south end. The train jumped and no one was in that part of the elevator.

The front of the engine lacked only a few feet of going clear through the building, part of the west side being pushed out by the impact. When it finally stopped, the engine was tilted at a sharp angle with the wheels on one side buried in the mud under the elevator. That part of the building was occupied by cleaning machinery, etc. being an addition to the original building. The machinery was wrecked, and a small quantity of grain was ruined. The beam held the upper story in place, and the big bins remained intact.

Traffic was blocked for 14 hours, it being 10:45 that night when the two wrecking crews and two of the road's largest cranes finally completed the task of hauling the prostrate engine out of the building, thus allowing the passage of trains through the side track. It was Tuesday morning before the main line was again opened.

The railroad is of course responsible for the loss to the elevator. Repairs are already underway. The engine was Number 1114, one of the largest on the road. It weighs 190 tons. It was placed on the track and hauled to the repair shop." (Photo courtesy of James Hilty and Evelyn Raskin Hilty.)

NEWARK POST OFFICE AND BALDWIN LAKE, BEHIND NEWARK. Very early in Holly Township's history, a community developed on the Holly-Flint Road at the top of the hill where it curved west to go around Baldwin Lake. Today, it is the intersection of North Holly Road and Belford Roads. The road has been straightened. A store, a school, and a church shared the same building there. Later, when the railroad was built, Newark was the location for a post office and grain elevator. The railroad station was called Belford and the post office was called South Grand Blanc. This led to some confusion. In 1909, the people of the area circulated a petition requesting that both be named Newark, after Newark, New Jersey. (Photos courtesy of Don Simons.)

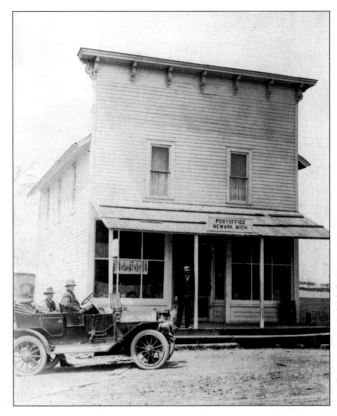

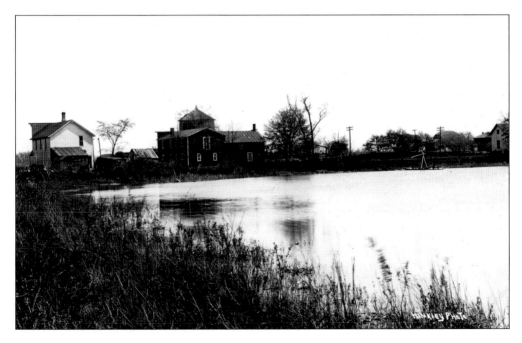

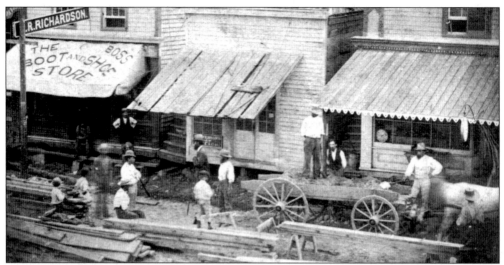

MARTHA STREET CONSTRUCTION, 1873. The caption on the back of the original photo states that this is Granddad Buzzell and his brother, Evans. Granddad is in the white shirt under the left end of the wooden awning. Martha Street was named after Ira C. Alger's daughter.

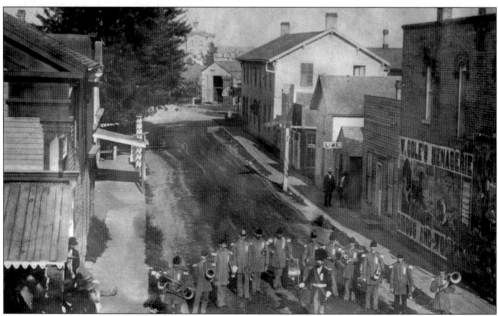

LOOKING EAST ON MARTHA STREET, 1874. The old Washington House may be seen on upper center of the photo. In the middle upper portion, just to the right of the branches of the tree, is the old Union School. In the foreground is a group of band men, identified from left to right: Will Baird, Sam Lobdell, Charles Burger, Nor Sherwood, Delos LeGrande Buell, Clint Sherwood, Mel Bowman, William Stone, Arthur Hadley, Charles Buzzell, and leader, Sidney Whalen.

After 1885, the name of the street one block east of South Saginaw was changed to Battle Alley because of a fight. The fight was between local young men and the crew of the circus. The circus crew was so badly beaten that they left town without unloading. In 1910, the donations of local merchants paid for a brick pavement on Battle Alley, Holly's first. The ruts and mud and hitching posts were abolished.

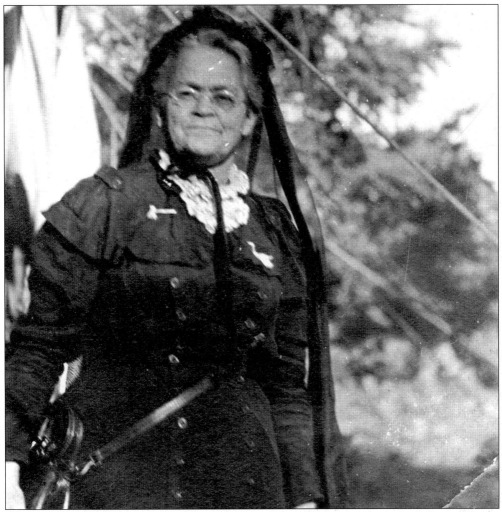

CARRY NATION. When the famous prohibitionist, Carry Nation, visited the town of Holly at the turn of the century, the village boasted the first railroad junction in Michigan. It was thriving area, with 100 to 120 trains passing through each day. Lumberjacks mingled with the new breed of men, the railroaders. Holly had 18 bars, which overflowed with customers. The streets were filled with battling, brawling men. Houses of ill repute were also present, tucked in amongst the bars.

Carry Nation was a woman who entered the public arena to protest all substance abuse and abuse of the laws of the land. Her first husband had a drinking problem and she ended up divorcing him. This event set the course for the rest of her life. The Kansas City woman arrived by train on August 29, 1908. Brought to the village by the County Prohibition Committee, she gave her lecture to the townspeople at the Baird Opera House.

After the talk, followed by a large group of people, Nation (who was a tall woman of tremendous girth) threw back her black cape and lifted her closed parasol. Holding her umbrella high, like a torchbearer, she entered the bars and swept her parasol from one end of the bar to the other. Many regarded her as a modern-day Joan of Arc.

For over 30 years, Holly has held the Carry Nation Festival on the weekend after Labor Day. It is a state-sanctioned annual festival and is embraced by the entire community; thousands of visitors attend. (Photo courtesy of James Hilty and Evelyn Raskin Hilty.)

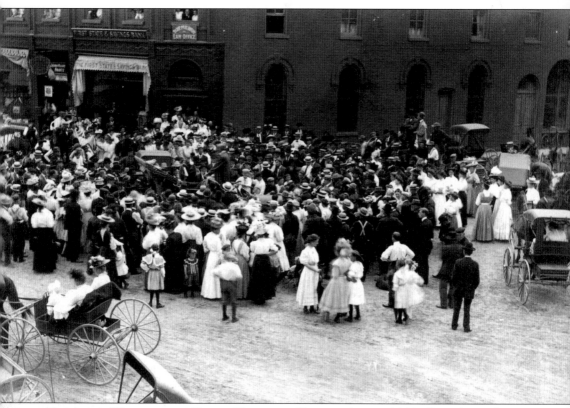

GOVERNOR WARNER AND CARRY NATION IN BATTLE ALLEY, 1908. Carry began her visit with an argument with the landlord at the Holly Inn, regarding an oil painting over the bar. The fight escalated and she was escorted out of the building. As reported in the *Holly Herald* from that time period, Nation accosted Governor Warner just as he was getting out of his automobile. He had been delivering a speech from his car on Saginaw Street. She wanted to know if he would remove the sheriff of Oakland County if he did not enforce the liquor law. The governor did not reply, but left instead. Nation said, "Now I am going to the Baird's Opera House to speak and if anyone wants to ask me a question, I will try and answer it and not sneak off like a coward."

After her speech at Baird's Opera House, she offered her little hatchet pins for sale. To this day, wooden hatchets are sold in commemoration of this event. Nation left town on the evening train to Detroit. Her parting words were said to have been that she had ". . . seen many worse towns than Holly!" (Photo courtesy of James Hilty and Evelyn Raskin Hilty.)

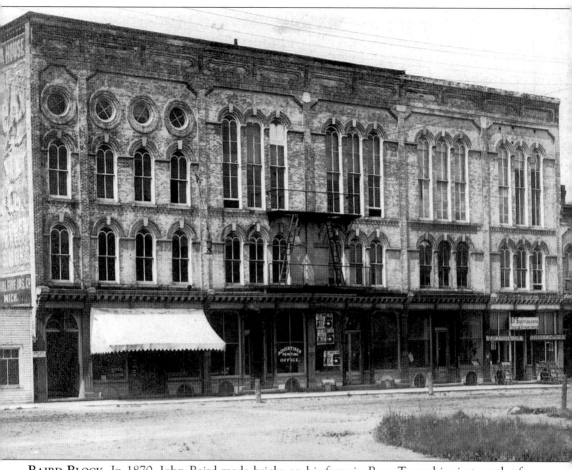

BAIRD BLOCK. In 1870, John Baird made bricks on his farm in Rose Township, just south of Holly. He built the three-and-one-half story Baird's Opera House with those bricks. George Schooley was the carpenter. The building was located north of the railroad tracks, on the west side of South Broad Street, and opened its doors in 1872. Originally, this was Holly's main street, with a hotel, saloon, and all kinds of shops. Only two of the original buildings still exist.

A wide three-flight grand stairway was at the south end of the building and narrow stairs were at the north end. The opera house covered the entire third floor, boasting a stage with painted scenery and a curtain embellished with local advertisements. There were footlights across the west end with a small balcony on the south wall. Two hundred and fifty wood chairs provided seating. There were grilled iron balconies outside the second- and third-story windows. The opera house was used for plays by traveling stock shows, vaudeville, medicine shows, lecture courses, revivals, and political rallies. Baird's was even used for roller skating and the "Electric Theatre" (better known as the movies); it was the scene of the annual formal Masonic and Firemen's Balls from 1877 to 1904. Located off the central second-floor hall were the first Masonic Lodge Odd Fellow and Rebecca rooms. These were later rented as flats. In 1912 and 1913, it was used for high school classrooms during the construction of the new high school. The upper floors were destroyed by fire in 1929. The lower part of the building is still in use.

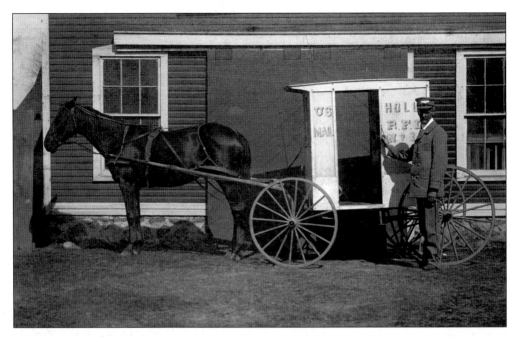

JIM STARKER, FIRST RURAL MAILMAN, AND RURAL MAIL CARRIERS OUTSIDE HALL, 1901.
Peter Fagan was instrumental in getting the post office located here and naming it "Holly Mills Post Office." It was a small one-story wooden building first located on the southeast corner of Saginaw and Sherman Streets. During the Civil War, a crowd gathered at noon each day to hear news of the war. In 1848, the hamlet became known as Holly. (Second photo courtesy of Bruce Dryer.)

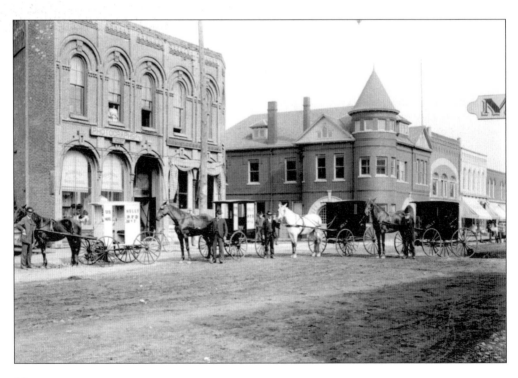

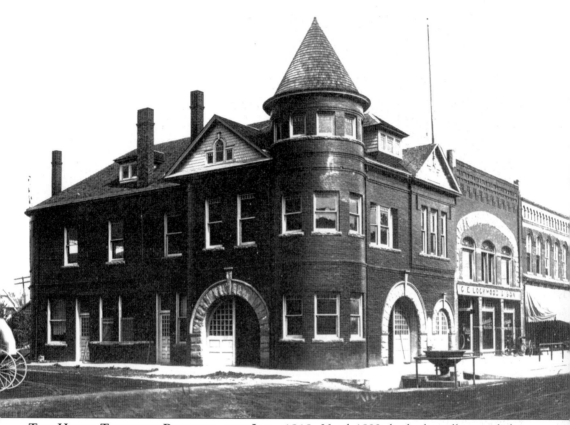

THE HOLLY TOWNSHIP BUILDING AND JAIL, 1918. Until 1892, both the village and the township held their monthly meetings in temporary locations. In April of 1899, the voters approved a resolution to build a town hall. It was not until 1891 that they finally passed a resolution to approve the site location. The township paid a total of $700 for the lot. The total cost of the building was $5,000. It is located on the northwest corner of south Saginaw and Front (Civic) Street.

Finally completed in August of 1892, the second floor was used for public meetings and as a voting place. The fire hose was hung in the corner for drying. It was also the storage area for the hose cart. The Volunteer Fire Department met there during a fire call to get equipment. At that time there were four wards, with a free fire telephone in each ward. The steam whistle at the Water Works blew a fire alarm to signal the ward. The first team or dray to arrive pulled the hose cart to the fire and was paid.

The jail cells were in the basement until an escaping prisoner became lodged in a furnace duct. Hobos who hopped trains looking for work were allowed night lodging if requested by the village marshall. A large cast-iron horse-watering trough was installed in front of the hall and left there until World War II, when it was melted down for the war effort. (Photo courtesy of Rick Holling.)

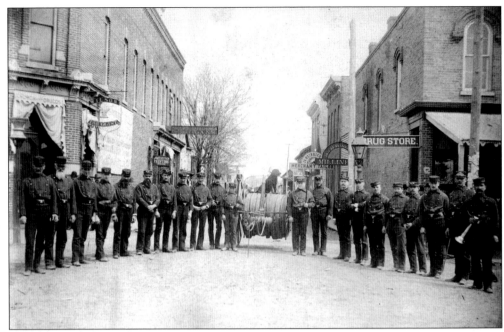

FIREMEN WITH HOSE, C. 1910. In 1880 the Holly Fire Department was established with a crew of one chief, one assistant chief, and ten regular men. The first fire equipment was built by the firemen themselves. In 1892, the Township Fire Hall was erected to house all of the village apparatus. (Photo courtesy Bruce Dryer.)

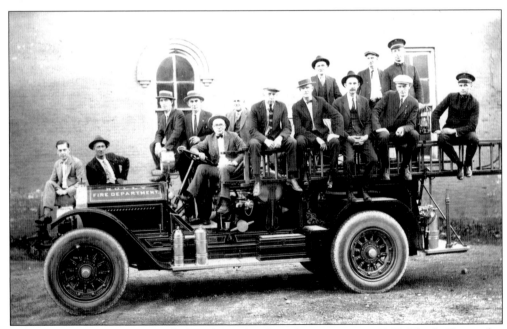

FIREMEN ON FIRE TRUCK. Holly bought its first horseless pumper in 1917. The LaFrance fire engine cost $40,000. In the past, firemen were paid $1 annually to volunteer, no matter how much they worked. Holly's 16 fire hydrants used Mill Pond water. (Photo courtesy of John and Suzanne Bianchette.)

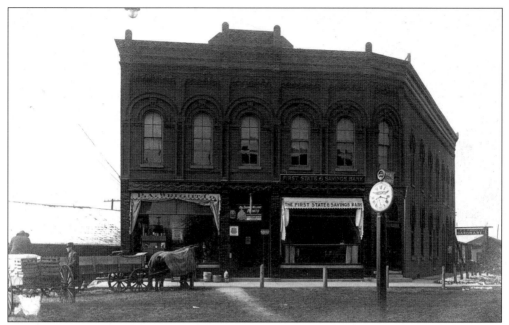

THE FIRST STATE SAVINGS BANK. Necessity became the mother of invention in 1866 when the first telephone line was installed by D.H. Stone, a local hotel owner, and C.A. Wilson, the cashier at the bank. Two tomato cans became receivers with a bladder stretched tightly over the can and a stout cord strung between their two places of business. By 1894, the primitive device was replaced by a switchboard system with Emma Sargent as its first operator. (Photo courtesy of James Hilty and Evelyn Raskin Hilty.)

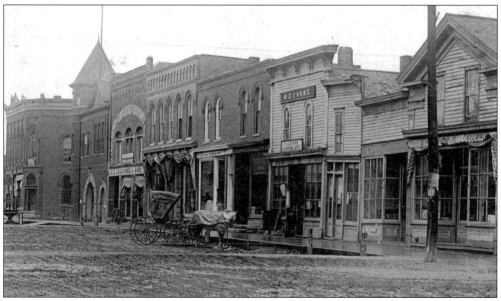

SAGINAW STREET, WEST SIDE, NORTH OF BANK CORNER. A series of fires in the 1870s destroyed all the wood frame buildings on Saginaw Street. These events spurred the construction of the first Water Works Building, next to the Mill Pond, in 1880. (Photo courtesy of Rick Holling.)

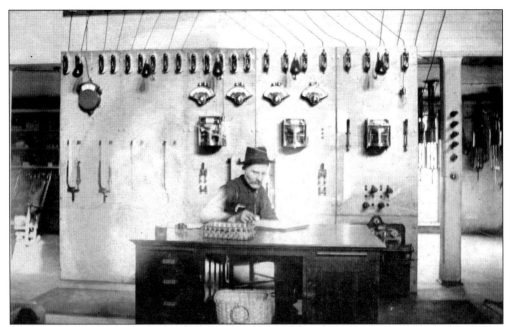

BROAD STREET WATER WORKS BUILDING INTERIOR. In 1880, two steam-powered pumps were installed in a 12-by-25-foot one-story wood and brick building. The tiny plot of land was leased for 99 years from M. Stiff. It was located on the west side of South Broad Street, south of the Mill Pond Dam, and it is still there today. Shown is Louis J. Striggow, the engineer, whose family has lived in Holly since 1864.

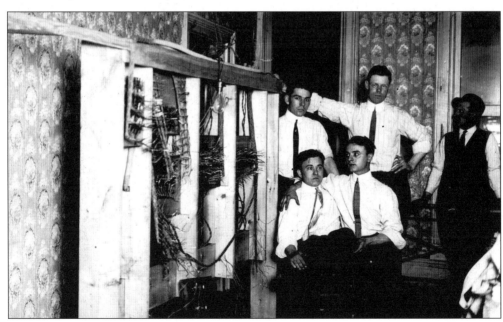

MOVING TELEPHONE WIRES, APRIL 24, 1913. The telephone came to town in 1894. Lines were strung into the outer township during the first decade after the turn of the century. Notes on the back of the photograph identify these men as Mr. Meisher, Mr. Campbell, Mr. Fisher, and Mr. Bridges. (Photo courtesy of David V. Tinder.)

Two
BUSINESSES

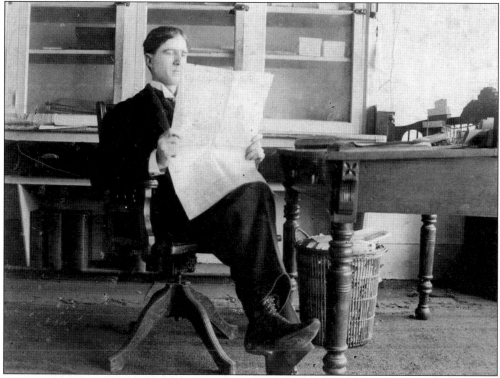

FRED PATTERSON, SR. In 1897, E.E. Patterson and his brother, Fred Patterson, took possession of the *Oakland Advertiser* from Fred Slocum. Fred bought out his brother's share of the paper in 1907, and from then on, Fred and his wife, Eliza, worked together. They published the *Advertiser* and changed the name to the *Holly Advertiser*. The Pattersons published the *Holly Advertiser* for 54 years. The Pattersons had two children, Elizabeth and George. George Patterson became a partner in the business in 1933, and after the death of his father, his name was listed as publisher.

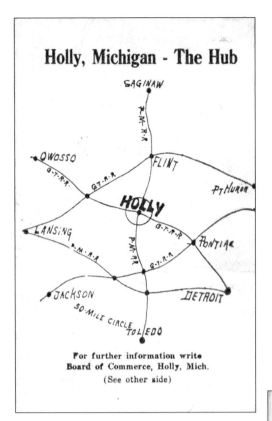

Holly, Michigan - The Hub

SAGINAW

P·M·R·R

QWOSSO

G·T·R·R

FLINT

G·T·R·R

HOLLY

PT HURON

LANSING

P·M·R·R

G·T·R·R

P·M·R·R

PONTIAC

G·T·R·R

JACKSON

50·MILE CIRCLE

DETROIT

TOLEDO

For further information write
Board of Commerce, Holly, Mich.
(See other side)

ADVERTISING HOLLY, THE HUB. The first Board of Commerce was formed in 1905. It was called the Holly Improvement Association. Members donated over $5,000 to a fund in hopes of luring industry to the village. Village taxpayers voted a matching bond levy for the same purpose. The village was in an ideal position to expand commercial and industrial interests.

In 1908, several businesses were encouraged to locate in the village, the most notable being the Hobart M. Cable Company—a piano factory later called the Grinnell Piano Factory—and the H.J. Heinz Pickle Factory. Both businesses were located at the east end of the Mill Pond. At that time it was recorded that over 200 men were employed in local industry. Agriculture and the railroads, however, were still the major employers in the area.

FACTS ABOUT HOLLY, MICH.

Excellent hotel.
Boulevard lights.
Five fine churches.
Unexcelled schools.
A $25,000 city hall.
Beautiful residences.
Two good newspapers.
Wide awake merchants.
A $100,000 bank building.
Annual pay roll, $850,000.
Business, $4,000,000 annually.
Two miles concrete pavement.
Fine manufacturing sites free.
Eighteen passenger trains daily.
Wide awake Board of Commerce.
Bank with resources of $1,800,000.
Many lodges and literary societies.
Abundant water and electric power.
Grand Trunk and Pere Marquette Rys.
Immense reservoir for fire protection.
City water supply drawn from wells.
Fine opportunity for profitable employment.
Unrivaled facilities as a manufacturing center.
Bonafide and profitable opportunities for investment of capital.
Come and see the biggest little city on earth.   (over)

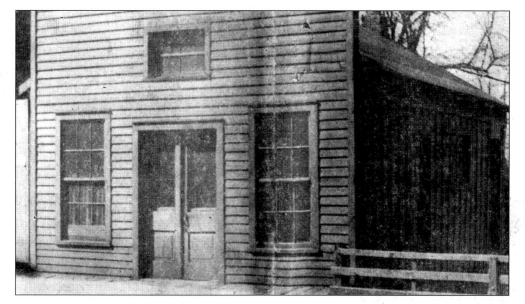

THE *HERALD* NEWSPAPER OFFICE, C. 1901 AND EXTERIOR OF THE *ADVERTISER*. Transportation and communication are two necessities when establishing communities. Holly and Michigan were once part of the old Northwest Territory. No town felt like a town until residents had established at least one newspaper. Holly and its environs were no exceptions.

The *Holly Register* was the first newspaper, established in 1865. Mr. Crawford was the first publisher; he then sold the paper after one year to E. Frank Blair. By 1869, the *Register* was resold to Henry Jenkins. For a short time, Holly also boasted the *Holly Circular*, started in 1872, and the *Holly Times*, established in 1875. These were both short-lived publications.

Joe Haas started the *Holly Herald* in September 1, 1901. He purchased the tinker shop, a small wooden building, shown above, and began publishing the *Holly Herald* with borrowed capital of $50. In 1914, he built a brick building to replace the old structure on Martha Street, later named Battle Alley. In 1939, the paper was sold to E.A. Stankrauff, and later, the Joe McCall family. (Top photo courtesy of the centennial edition of the *Holly Herald*.)

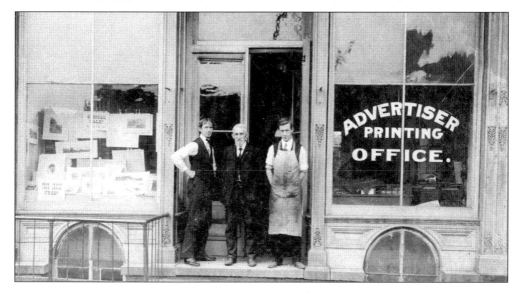

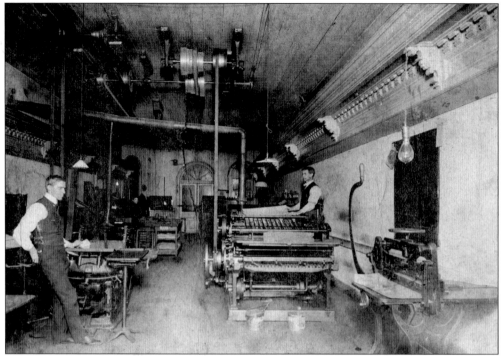

NEWSPAPER PRINTING PRESS. The *Holly Herald* newspaper was printed on this printing press. It printed only two pages at a time, and the paper then had to be fed through the press again, to print the backside. The operators stood at the back of the press and slid the single sheet through the press. The operators worked so mechanically that they literally went to sleep on the press.

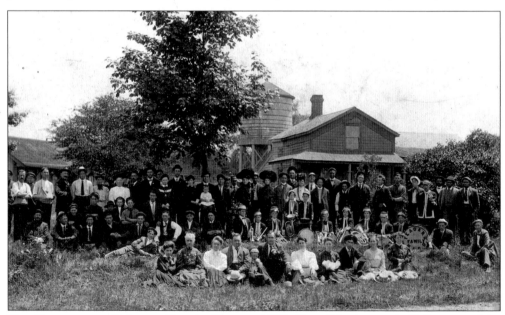

THE BAND OF THE FEANGAN FAMILY CIRCUS, 1902. Not all businesses in Holly were of the conventional variety. The Feangan Family Circus troupe is pictured here on Sherman Street in 1905. They lived in Holly when not traveling with Wickes Circus via the railroad lines.

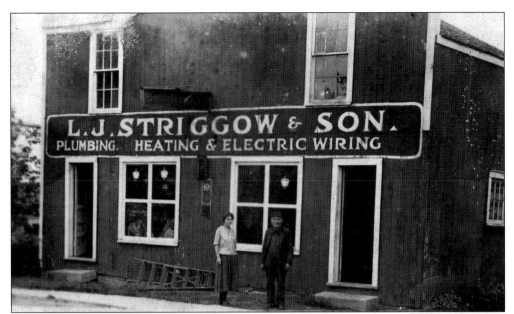

L.J. STRIGGOW AND SON. In 1880, Lewis J. Striggow became Holly's first fire chief, with 19 volunteers. Later, he became an electrical engineer at the Holly Water Works. Lew began a plumbing business in 1912 in the basement of the two-story cement block building. In 1916, he bought this wooden shop structure, built by a wagon and carriage maker. He went into general contracting with his son, Justin, specializing in plumbing, heating, and electrical work. (Photo courtesy of Terry Striggow.)

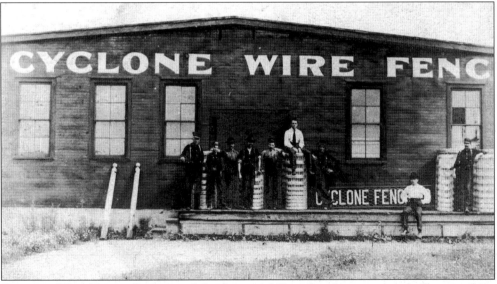

CYCLONE WIRE FENCE COMPANY. John Lane and Cornelius Lane invented a fence-making machine on their family farm around 1887. By twisting three or four cables into woven stays three or four inches apart, very similar to snow fencing, the machines made good, strong fences. Around 1890, the Lane brothers had developed a machine that could be sold to a farmer to weave the fencing right in the field. East of Grant Street and the Pere Marquette Railroad, the brothers erected a large one-story corrugated iron-sided factory.

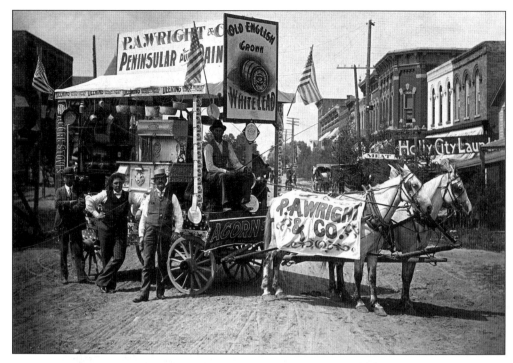

P.A. Wright & Co. Wagon and **P.A. Wright Hardware Store.** Originally, the Wright family began their hardware business in Davisburg, a farming community southeast of Holly. Porter Wright bought out his brother's share in 1897. During the winter of 1900, he acquired the inventory of the W. Holmes and Company hardware store in Holly. He finally settled on a Saginaw Street location, next to the township hall, after trying three other buildings. (Second photo courtesy of James Hilty and Evelyn Raskin Hilty.)

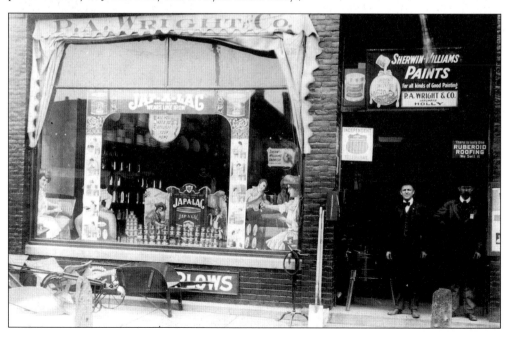

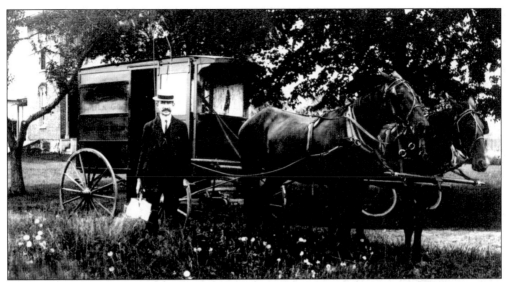

HENNING AND SHIELDS MILK COMPANY. Henning and Shields was one of the first companies to home-deliver milk in this area. Presentation was important, so the carriage and horses and milkman were all dressed for the job. (Photo courtesy of James Hilty and Evelyn Raskin Hilty.)

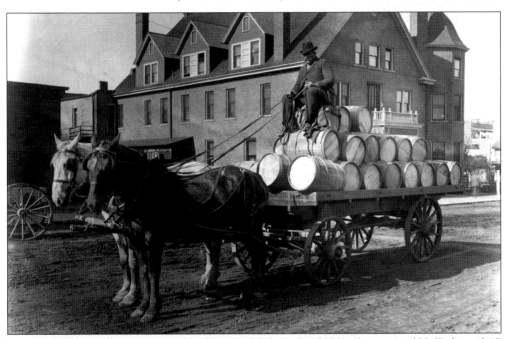

FRANCES HADLEY DELIVERS TO THE HOTEL. Back in the 1800s, the town of Holly hosted 17 hotels. It was said that Broad Street was the main section of town, followed by Martha Street, and then Saginaw Street. The Hodsky House was the first Holly hotel and was built by Leicester Hodsky in the 1850s, serving the town for 13 years. Then the hotel was sold to John T. Andrews. It was located on the southwest corner of Broad and Sherman, with the cost for one night's lodging at $1. The Home Hotel was built on South Broad Street in 1867 by Justin Coon. The name was changed to the Teeple Hotel and later to the Exchange Hotel. Francis Hadley is shown delivering kegs of beer to the Hirst Hotel. Today that hotel is known as the Holly Hotel.

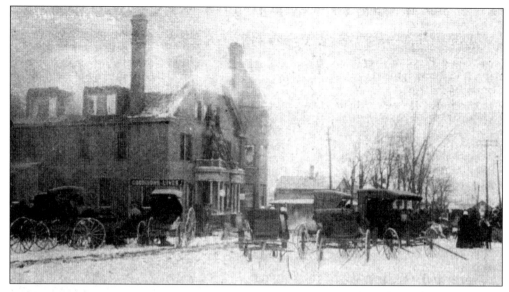

HIRST HOTEL FIRE, 1913, AND THE ALLENDORF HOTEL. In 1860, the old wood Washington House Hotel stood at this site. In 1891, John Hirst built a fine brick three-story hotel. It was stylishly furnished, the parlor on the south side had gold brocade upholstered furniture and white rose figured Brussels carpeting. The dining room extended the length along the Martha Street side, with a dumbwaiter in the rear to bring liquor up from the basement. Local game and fish were served. Two- or three-course dinners were available for 30¢ or 50¢ on linen tablecloths with fine china, crystal, silverware, and finger bowls. The hotel featured electric lights, furnace heating, a tonsorial parlor (barbershop) and public bathing in the basement. The area was also used as a display room for traveling salesmen. In 1913, the building burned and was rebuilt. It became known as the Holly Inn by 1919. It later became the Allendorf, the Norton, and then the Holly Hotel. (Bottom photo courtesy of Don Simons.)

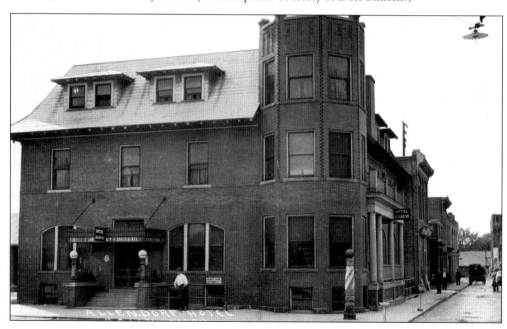

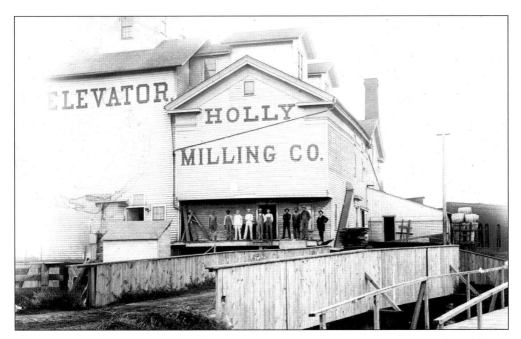

HOLLY MILLING COMPANY. In 1875, the mill employed 10 men. They turned out 150 barrels of flour a day with a capacity of 200 barrels. A railroad siding reached the mill located near the Water Works. Gradually as the village grew with the railroad, so did the mill. "Holly Velvet" flour became a nationally-distributed product and for several years was exported to Europe. One year, during a famine, nearly the entire production was shipped to Russia.

By the time the building burned down, the factory was running 2 shifts a day with 50 men each. At that point they were shipping 300 to 400 barrels of flour daily. For weeks after the mill caught fire on December 17, 1910, 6,000 bushels of wheat burned, with a loss of $50,000.

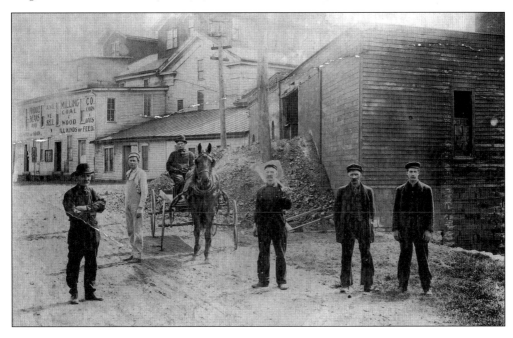

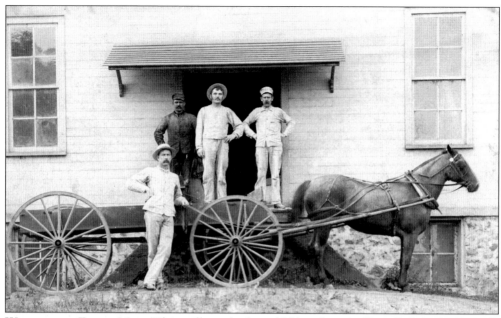

WINGLEMIRE FLOUR MILL. This mill was built in 1884 and originally called the Holly Mill. The building was located on the southeast corner of Oakland and First Street. John Joslin is pictured in the front row. In the back row, pictured from left to right are the following: Henry Cook, engineer; Charles DeLonge; and William Reed, partner in the mill.

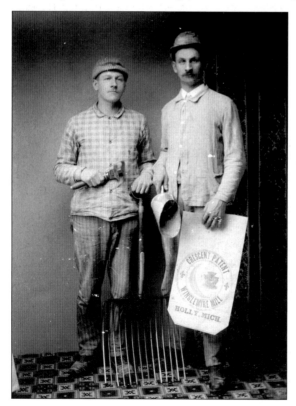

WINGLEMIRE FLOUR MILL EMPLOYEES. At left is John Copp, an employee, and at right is Joseph P. Winglemire Jr., manager. Joe Winglemire is holding a flour bag for Crescent Patented Flour, which was the Winglemire brand name. He lived across the street at 102 Oakland. (Photo courtesy of Don Winglemire.)

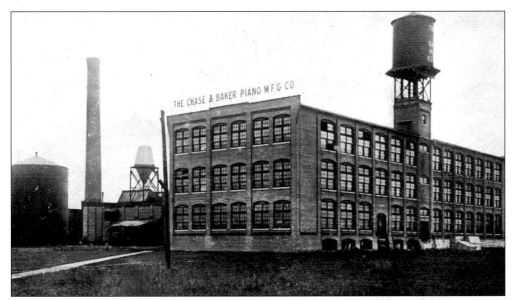

CHASE & BAKER PIANO MANUFACTURING COMPANY. This post card is of the Chase & Baker Piano Factory Company. The massive three-story building with a water tower on the roof and separate one-story brick fuel and boiler room was finished by the Hobart M. Cable Company in 1907. It was located on the south side of the Grand Trunk Railroad, on the east side of Cogshall Street. (Photo courtesy of Don Simons.)

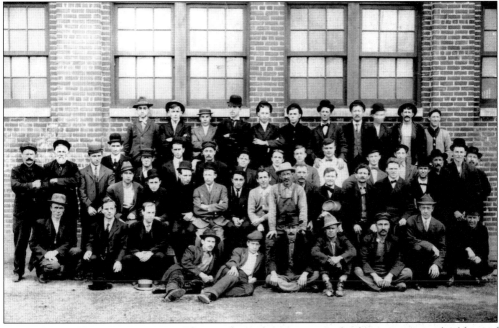

H.M. CABLE EMPLOYEES, 1908. This modern plant consists of a four-story main building of brick construction, offices, mill room, dry kiln room, and steam engine room. The business employed approximately 50 people. In 1913, brothers Clayton and Leonard Grinnell bought the plant and called it Grinnell Brothers Piano Company. The factory produced grand, upright, and player pianos, and benches from start to finish.

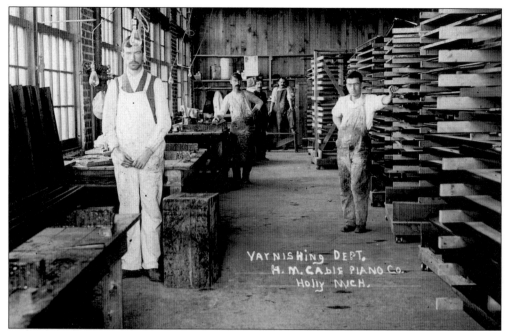

PIANO PRODUCTION, VARNISHING DEPARTMENT. Many old-world craftsmen came to work in the factory and stayed on because they liked the community. Piano styles changed during a half-century, but the method of manufacturing has made only a few changes. (Photo courtesy of David V. Tinder.)

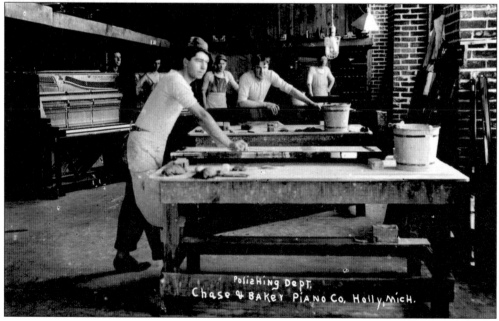

PIANO PRODUCTION, POLISHING DEPARTMENT. In this time period, the cabinetry work was done by hand. Although modern equipment is used to prepare the wood today, it is still necessary for skilled hands to assemble the delicate mechanism and to put the final touches on the cabinet. (Photo courtesy of David V. Tinder.)

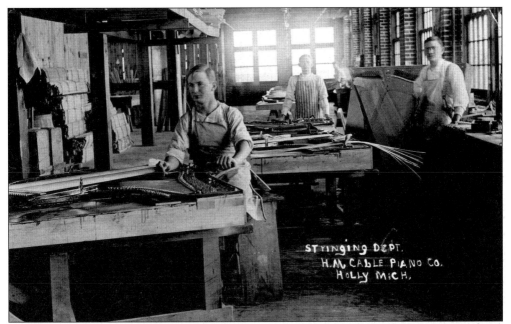

PIANO PRODUCTION, STRINGING DEPARTMENT. The pull of the strings equals the weight of 20 tons or more. The piano has three times as many moving parts as an automobile. (Photo courtesy of David V. Tinder.)

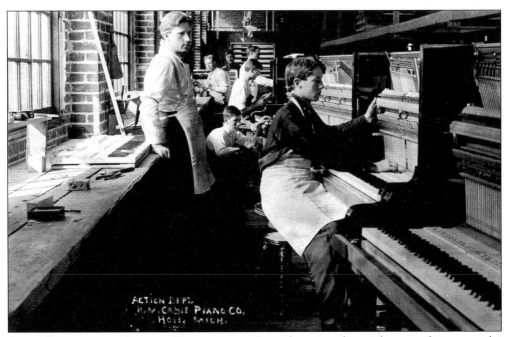

PIANO PRODUCTION, ACTION DEPARTMENT. Over the years, the production of pianos at the Holly factory was increased to meet the demands of the growing chain of Grinnell Music Stores. Further demands were placed on the factory in Holly when it eventually became the only piano factory of Grinnell Brothers. (Photo courtesy of David V. Tinder.)

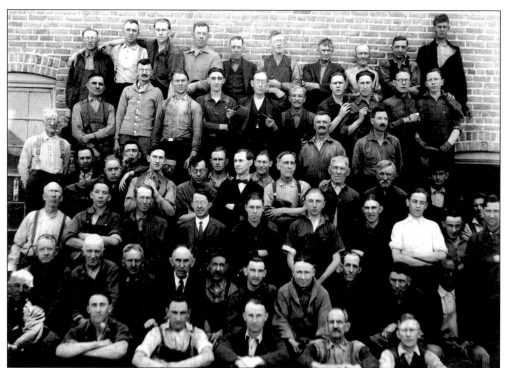

H.M. Cable Employees, Continued. At one time, Grinnell Brothers employed more than 100 employees and produced 2,500 fine pianos a year. Many were skilled mechanics and stayed with the company until they retired. It was considered the largest piano factory in the world and was sold in 1970. (Photo courtesy of Bruce Dryer.)

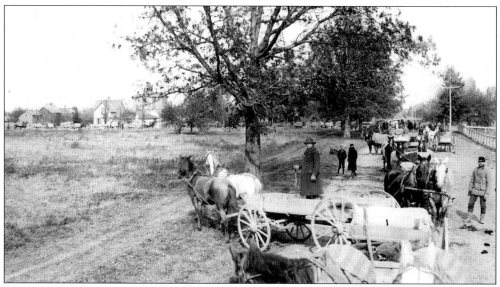

Wagons at Holly Cider Mill, 1896. Farmers brought their harvested apples by wagon to the Holly Cider Mill. During the fall, they would sometimes leave their wagons overnight and then would come back the following day. Farmers respected each others' property. (Photo courtesy of Don Simons.)

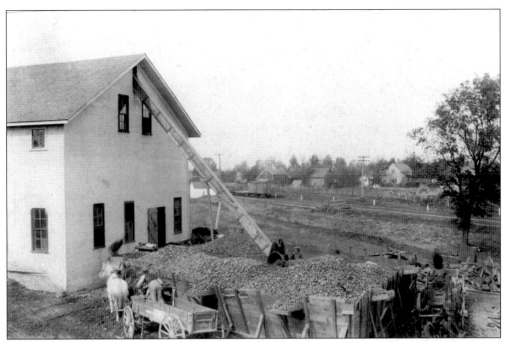

HOLLY CIDER MILL, 1896. The farmers would get 15¢ for every 100 pounds of apples delivered to the Holly Cider Mill. This and the previous photograph were taken from the photo scrapbook of C.A. Damon at the Hadley House Museum. (Photo courtesy of Don Simons.)

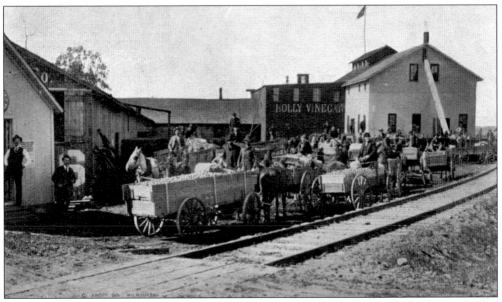

MAKING CIDER, POSTMARK 1907. Note the sign that says Holly Vinegar in the background. This was the location for both the Cider Mill and Vinegar Plant. (Photo courtesy of Don Simons.)

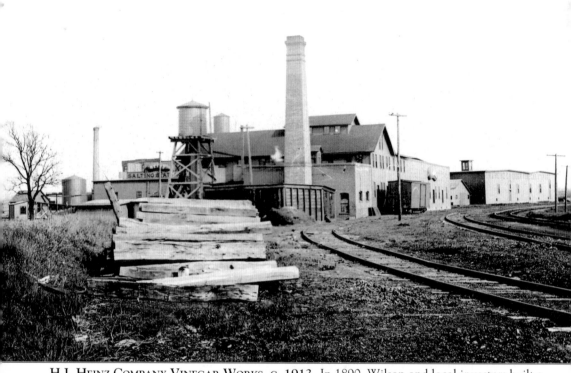

H.J. Heinz Company Vinegar Works, c. 1913. In 1890, Wilson and local investors built a cider mill and feed mill for their hog farm at the south end of Cogshall Street, south of the Grand Trunk Western Railroad and east of the C&O Railroad tracks. In 1896, the H.J. Heinz Company purchased the business. Enlarged, it became the world's largest vinegar and pickle salting plant. The long, wooden, one-story building was painted yellow with a large green trademark pickle. The building extended south along the Pere Marquette (C&O) railroad tracks and could be seen by passengers on all trains as they stopped before crossing the junction. Local farmers raised cucumbers from Heinz seed on contract. The farmers also sold 1,200 tons of apples daily during the season.

The factory employed two shifts of 50 men each. In 1909, Heinz moved to Muscatine, Iowa. The company returned in 1910 and operated here until 1931. (Photo courtesy of James Hilty and Evelyn Raskin Hilty.)

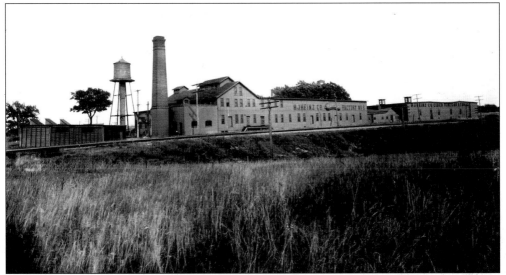

HEINZ PICKLE FACTORY NO. 5. The factory was located where the trains crossed and people could look at the green pickle on the building. After the building closed, young boys got the pickle off the building and used it for a raft on the old Mill Pond. It now rests someplace at the bottom of the pond.

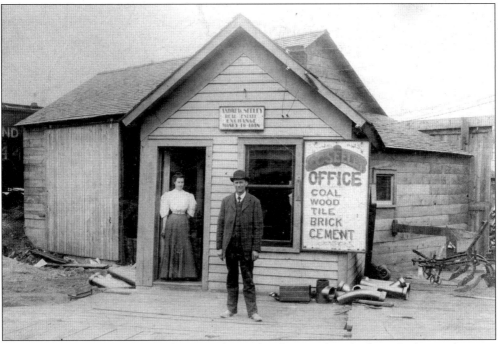

C.C. SEELEY COAL OFFICE. The sign above the door reads: "Andrew Seeley, real estate, exchange, money to loan." This building was the original first post office that was located at the southeast corner of Sherman and South Saginaw streets. It was then moved to the west side of Saginaw Street north of the Grand Trunk track. It became the office of the C.C. Seeley Coal and Wood Yard. Goldie Halstead Sherwood wrote, "C.C. Seeley, after reaching his goal, retired and went south where they do not need coal."

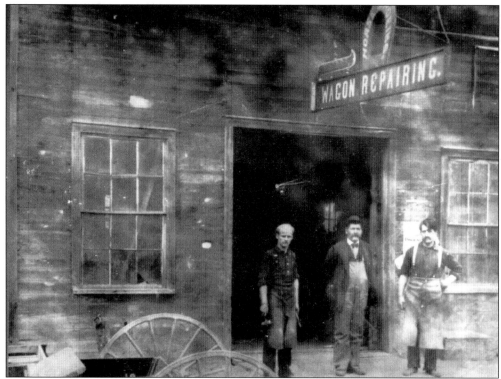

WAGON AND BLACKSMITH SHOP. This photo was taken around 1904. The building stood to the south on North Saginaw, about where the Winglemire store now stands. At left is "Smithy" Cass B. Waters and at right is his cousin, Herbert Walters. The bystander is not identified. Cass cared for the horses of James A. Bailey from the Barnum & Bailey Circus. In later years, Cass recalled, "I liked horse shoeing in those days and I would like it even now." (Photo courtesy of Bruce Dryer.)

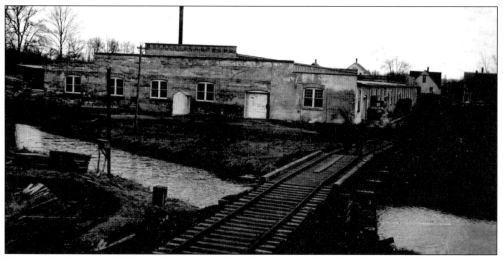

WAGON WORKS, C. 1907. Wagons pulled by horses were the chief method of transportation in this era. The manufacture and repair of wagons was essential for the livelihood of the townspeople. The Wagon Works was an important local industry. (Photo courtesy of James Hilty and Evelyn Raskin Hilty.)

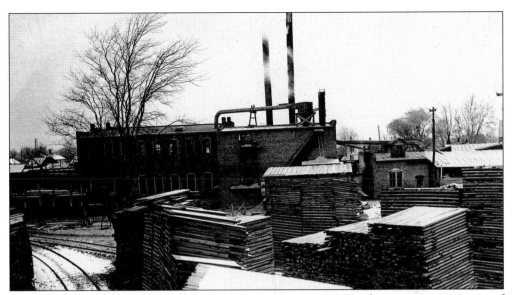

MICHIGAN MANUFACTURING AND LUMBER COMPANY, C. 1907. Lumber companies were one of the chief early businesses in Holly. The lumber industry was booming and the town was growing. Materials were needed for building. Because Holly had a railroad junction, dealers were able to ship lumber all over the state. (Photo courtesy of James Hilty and Evelyn Raskin Hilty.)

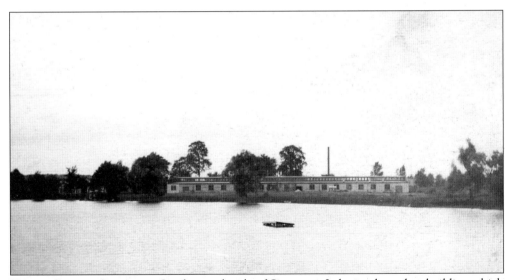

YOUNG SPRING COMPANY. On the north side of Simonson Lake is a long, low building which houses the American Spring and Manufacturing Corporation. In 1920, the company purchased the plant from L.A. Young. The building had been remodeled, but never used. American Spring made springs of every size and type, as well as wire specialties. This hardware was used in automobiles and agricultural implements.

49

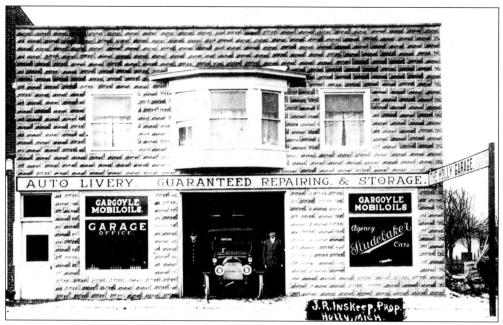

THE HOLLY GARAGE, C. 1910. At the turn of the century, J.R. Innskeep built a two-story cement block building at the corner of Maple and Saginaw. He lived upstairs and had his business downstairs. He specialized in automobile sales and also automobile rentals, with the option of including a driver. (Photo courtesy of the Holly Downtown Development Authority.)

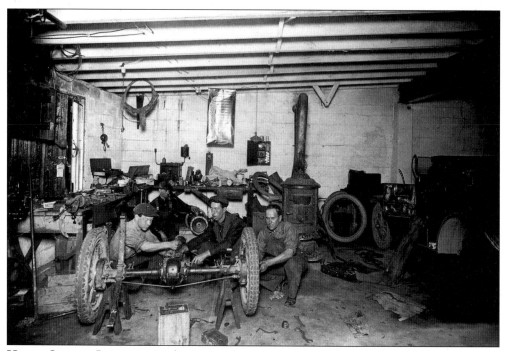

HOLLY GARAGE INTERIOR. In this image, four auto mechanics are hard at work repairing the rear axle of an automobile. The reason the wheels are so large is that the cars had to use the same unpaved roads that were originally used by horse-drawn wagons.

50

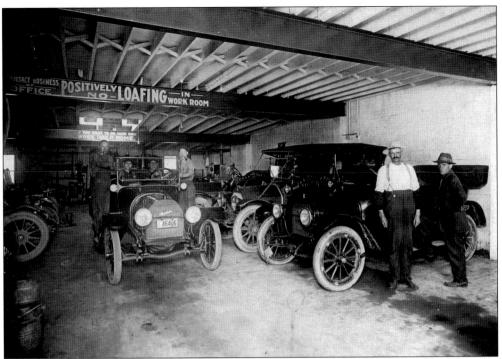

HOLLY GARAGE INTERIOR. The sign overhead reads: "Transact business at office" and "Positively no loafing in work room." Some of the garage was used for the display of new automobiles, while other areas were for repair.

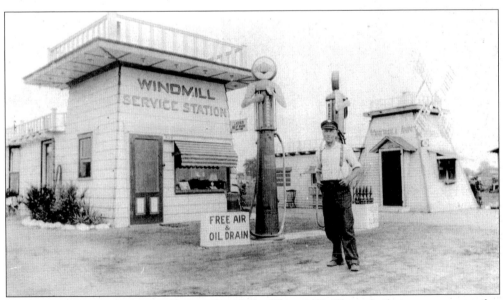

WINDMILL SERVICE STATION. During the 1930s, Clayton C. Klemp built a one-story wooden store and gas station with a large wooden windmill, as a landmark, on the roof. The Windmill Gas Station was located on the south corner of Lakeview and North Saginaw Streets. There were also cabins as part of the complex. (Photo courtesy of the Holly Downtown Development Authority.)

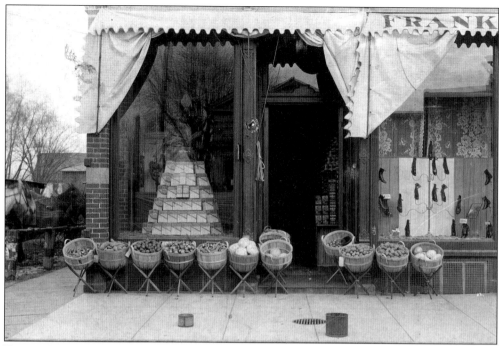

FRANK, MARKS, AND MARKS STORE. In a general store, it was not unusual to find groceries in the front and dry goods in the back. On the left side of the photograph is a railing with horses tied to it. There is a sidewalk but no paved street.

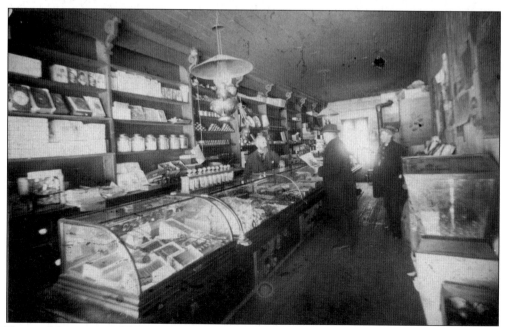

FRANK, MARKS, AND MARKS STORE, INTERIOR. In a general store, the customer had to ask for what he or she wanted, which was either inside a case or on shelves behind a counter. There was no such thing as self-serve. This prevented the goods from being handled excessively, thus protecting the inventory, which might remain in the store for some time.

FRANK, MARKS, AND MARKS STORE, FABRIC FOR SALE. In the back of this store was a dry goods area where bolts of fabric were on display. The customer could comfortably sit on a stool and examine the many examples of calico, cotton, linen, and wool. Inspired by the selection, the lady of the house would have been adept at sewing clothes for the entire family, as well as household furnishings, bed linens, and towels.

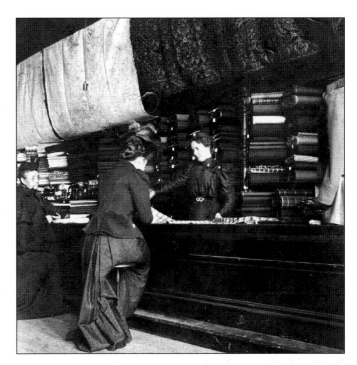

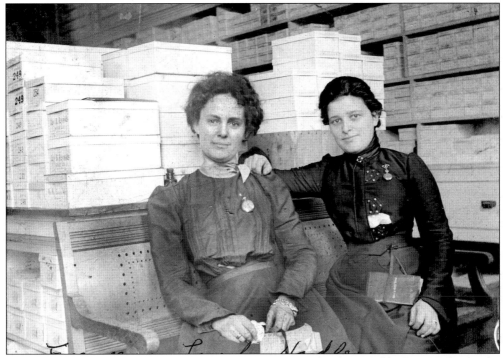

EMMA LAMB HADLEY AND ETTA MARKS. Over the years, shopkeepers like Etta Marks, on the right, developed close relationships with their patrons. It would not have been unusual to spend a morning or afternoon with a patron who was also a friend. In the background are boxes of shoes. The customer would have had their feet measured for the perfect fit.

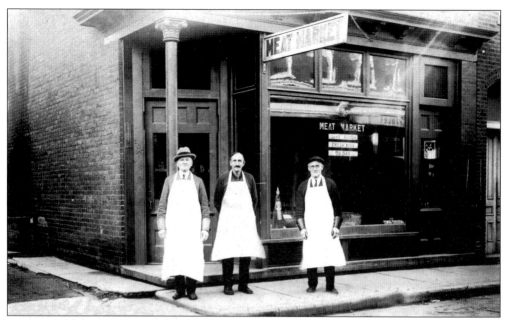

JARRARD MEAT MARKET. On the back of this photograph, there is a caption that reads: "Babcock made this picture for his brother-in-law, George. Worked some. Left Frank Jarrard. I worked here too, before going to farm in 1923—made sausage. On the left, Jarrard ran flour mill just off M-59 NE of Milford Road before he started this market in Battle Alley, Holly. This must have been about 1922 or 1923. In the center is Dad, George Downing. Right is Alvin Buck from Fenton." The Holly Inn Hotel was to the left of this building.

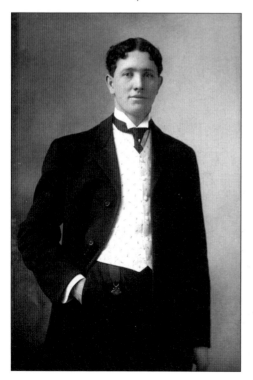

HARRY C. GORDON. Harry Gordon was born in Rose Township, south of Holly, on October 15, 1879. He came to the village in 1899 and was a clerk in the Nicholson Hardware Store. In 1903, he moved to the John D. Haddon Clothing Store as a clothing salesman. Goldie Halstead Sherwood wrote in 1938, "Gordon, a clothier of great renown, sells shirts, collars, and ties in our little town."

ISLA HAYES' PORTRAIT AND HAYES SHOE REPAIR SHOP. Albert and Isla Hayes repaired shoes in the days when it was easier and cheaper to repair an old pair of shoes than replace them. When Albert died in 1956, Isla continued repairing shoes alone. A sign displayed in the store proclaimed: "I can't milk your cow, I can't hold your baby, but I can save soles, and I don't mean maybe." All the tools and sign are on display at the Hadley House Museum. (Bottom photo courtesy of Bruce Dryer.)

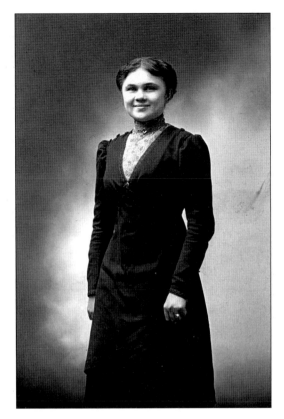

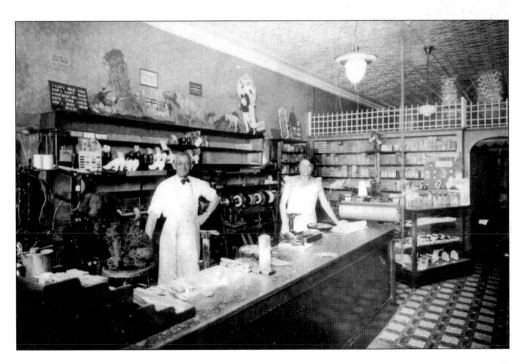

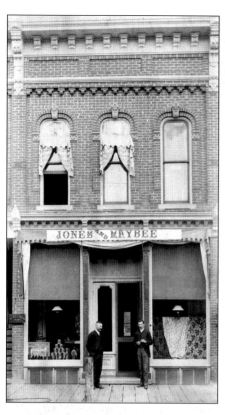

JONES & MAYBEE GENERAL STORE. Taking a break outside are James R. Jones (left) and John Maybee, owners of the store at 109 South Saginaw Street. Dr. Felshaw's office was upstairs.

BOWEN'S GROCERY AND SEELEY'S HARDWARE STORES. These buildings were located on the corner of Maple and Saginaw Streets. The dirt streets have given way to pavement.

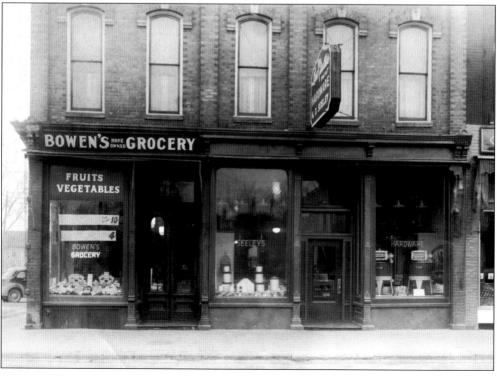

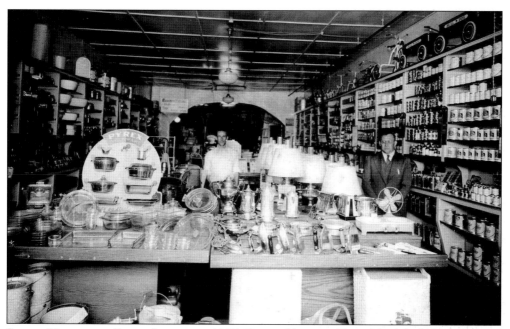

SEELEY HARDWARE STORE INTERIOR, 1935. Pictured here are Emory Gudith (left) and Henry D. Seeley, hardware storeowner. H.D. Seeley was active in the community and chaired the centennial parade committee. He belonged to the Holly High Alumni Association and served as their treasurer at one time.

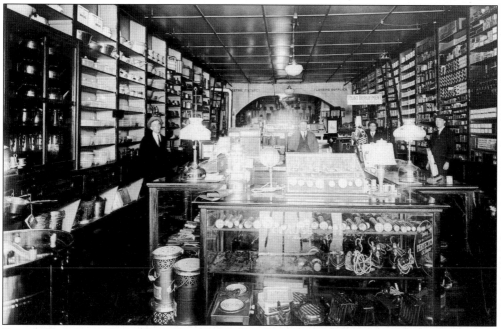

SEELEY HARDWARE STORE INTERIOR, 1935. An ad in the centennial anniversary edition of the *Holly Herald*, 1938, shows a farmer and reads: "It may have taken him longer to get to town . . . but he knew quality then, just as our customers do now." Seeley's Hardware carried "Clauss cutlery, Lowe Brothers paints and varnishes, Renown stoves and ranges, and good hardware of all kinds."

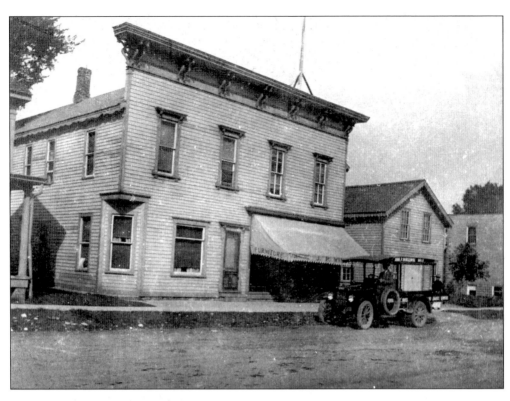

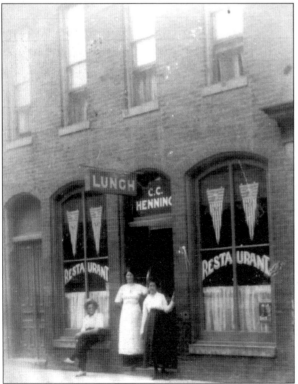

WINGLEMIRE FURNITURE STORE. Winglemire Furniture was founded in 1858 by Joseph P. Winglemire. The building pictured here was built in 1865 and is currently Joseph's Oak Shop. Also pictured is the first delivery truck with John P. Winglemire as the driver. The store is one of Michigan's oldest centennial businesses, run by the same family for 146 years. (Photo courtesy of Don Winglemire.)

HENNINGS RESTAURANT. The original structure that housed this restaurant was built in the late 1800s. This photo is from the late 1930s. Bruce Dryer used to sell his leftover newspapers in the restaurant as a teenager. His mother would take one sniff of him and say, "You've been at Hennings again." (Photo courtesy of Bruce Dryer.)

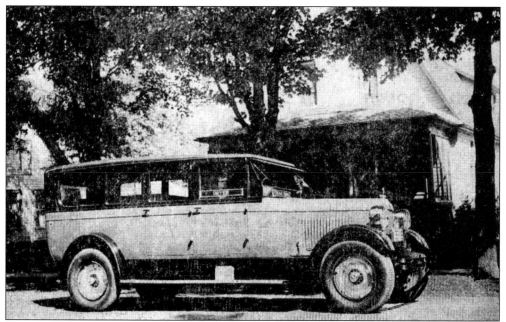

DRYER FUNERAL HOME. This image shows the first Dryer Funeral Home, located on Oakland Street, with the first hearse. Paul Dryer came to Holly in 1910 and was originally employed at the Grinnell Factory. In April of 1925, Dryer announced that he was becoming a funeral director and the Dryer family business continues on to this day. "Dryer the undertaker shows so much skill," wrote Goldie Halstead Sherwood, "he makes folks look natural when they are quite still." (Photo taken from the *Holly Advertiser*.)

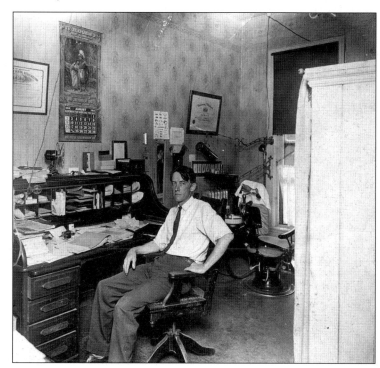

DR. JAMES CLARK.
Dr. Clark was a dentist with a Battle Alley office. He is shown here at his desk, with his dental chair and equipment in the background.

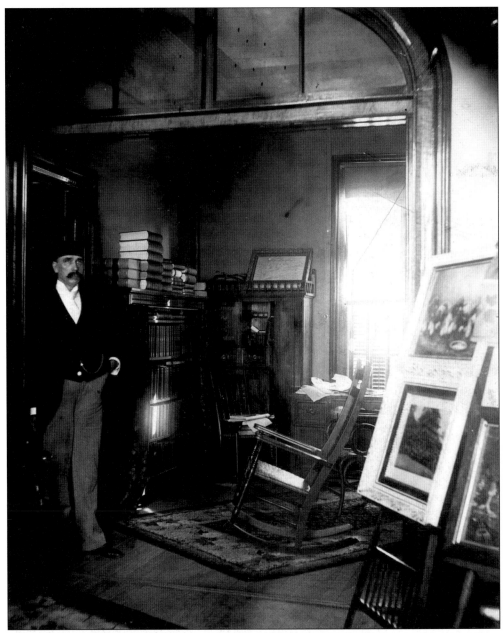

D.W.C. WADE, M.D. Dr. Wade came to Holly in February of 1861 and practiced medicine here for 42 years. A leading surgeon, his office was located at the corner of Washington and Maple.

He had been offered several other Michigan sites in which to practice, some in larger cities, but preferred to stay in Holly. Dr. Wade felt his friends were here and they needed him. Over the years he continued to study and keep up to date on all the new advances in medicine. For many years he was the surgeon for the Grand Trunk Railroad.

He was instrumental in the location of the old Holly High School, the building of the Town Hall, and the water works system. Mrs. Wade was also instrumental in forming the Ladies Library Association, the basis for the public library.

Three
STREET SCENES

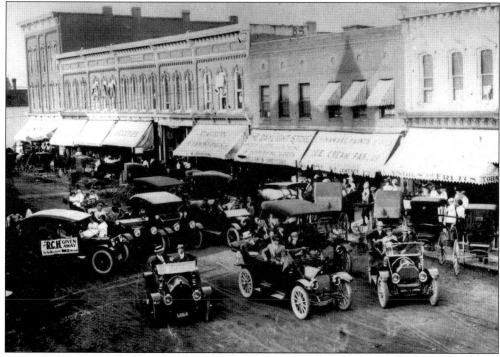

HANG YOUR HAT IN HOLLY. The first Booster Day took place July 3, 1913. This photograph was taken of the parade on the east side of South Saginaw Street. There was a raffle for a R.W.H. Touring Car. Local resident "Happy" Harry Smith of Cogshall Street won the raffle. Tickets were sold by merchants for 50¢ in trade.

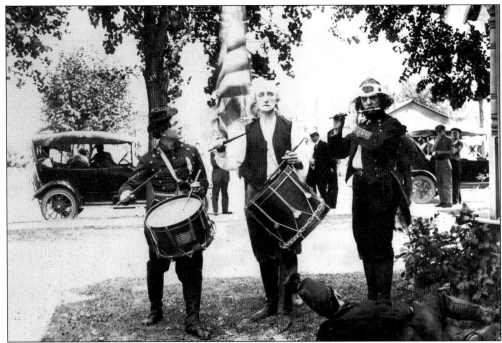

PARADE WARM-UP. Imitating a marching band from the Revolutionary War, this group led the way for the parade. The person at left is unidentified; Fenton Beebe is on the drum in the middle; and N.W. Wade is a wounded soldier playing a flute.

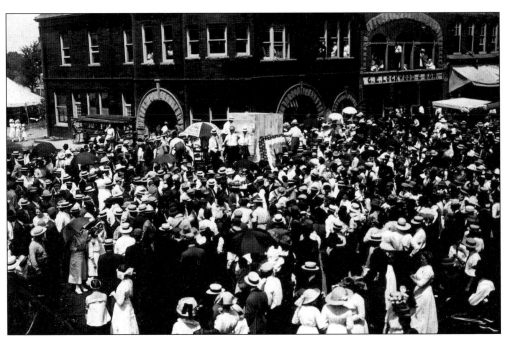

BOOSTER DAY CROWD. Everybody showed up for the parade and raffle on Booster Day, July 3, 1913. Merchants set up booths to sell food and souvenirs. As was the practice in those days, streamers and bunting were hung from the buildings and everyone displayed the American flag.

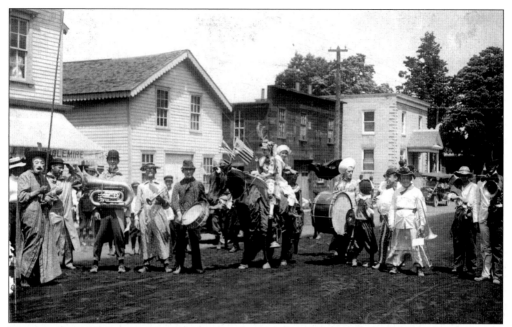

BOOSTER DAY HOODLUM BAND. The parade started on the north end of Saginaw Street and marched south. Pictured is the Hoodlum Band, which was made up of clowns, and those dressed in other costumes. Pictured in the center are two girls on a horse.

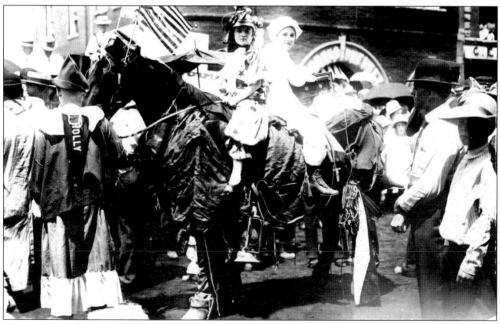

FIRST PRIZE. These girls, one riding the horse backwards, won first prize for their part in the Hoodlum Band. There was a judging booth in front of the Town Hall. This event was sponsored by the local merchants to promote business in the downtown area.

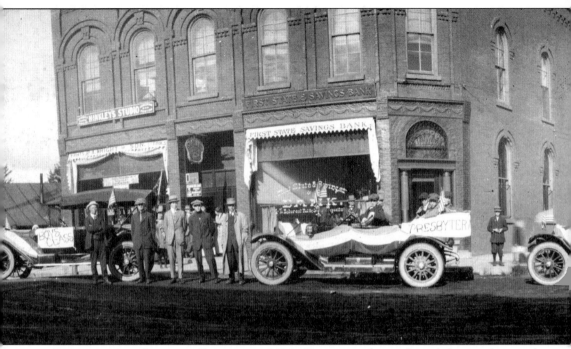

PANORAMA OF SAGINAW STREET, C. 1920. Businesses shown from left to right are the following: Hinkley's Studio, one of the local photographers; the Shoe Repair; the First State Savings Bank; and, across the street, the Township Hall. The people in Holly loved a parade.

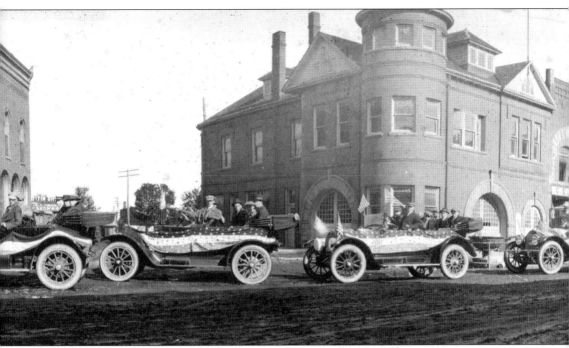

The decorated cars include the Boys' Class (left), the Presbyterian Church (middle), and the Sunday school (right).

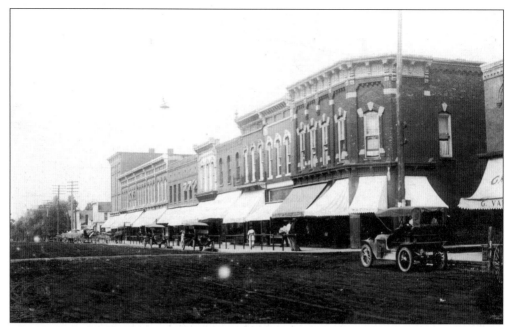

EAST SIDE, LOOKING NORTH ON SAGINAW STREET, C. 1910–1920. This Hinkley photograph shows the old horse hitching post, still in evidence next to the sidewalk. The street is still unpaved. Saginaw Street is so named because it was part of the Saginaw Trail. There are also Saginaw Streets in the Michigan cities of Pontiac, Flint, and Saginaw. (Photo courtesy of James Hilty and Evelyn Raskin Hilty.)

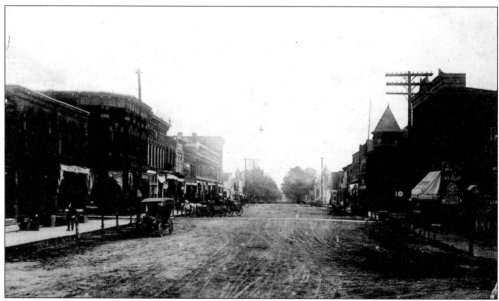

LOOKING SOUTH ON SAGINAW STREET. Oops! This is really a photograph of Saginaw Street looking north, but when the photograph was printed the negative was backwards. This is a test to see if you have paying attention and reading the captions. (Photo courtesy of Jim Hilty and Evelyn Raskin Hilty.)

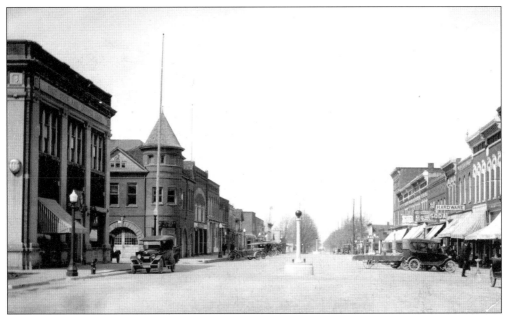

SAGINAW STREET, LOOKING NORTH, POSTMARK OCTOBER 29, 1928. This post card was sent to Mrs. Charles Travis. Some of the note reads: "Dear Mother, I got here about 10:30 and everything is alright. I work three hours this afternoon, but it sure was cold to work outdoors. But I like it there." It is signed A. Almore Ellis. There have been some changes to Saginaw Street, including a directional post to guide cars to the right side of the street.

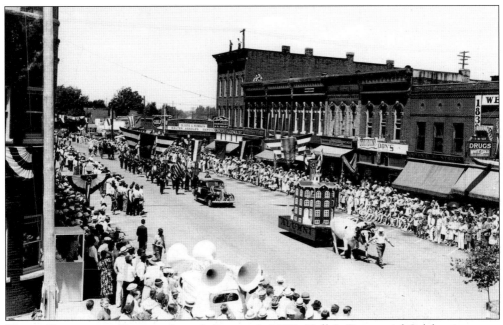

HOLLY CENTENNIAL PARADE, JULY 2, 3, AND 4, 1938. Holly's Centennial Celebration was a three-day event. There were many committees formed to put a proper face on the party. A special official souvenir program book was produced at the price of 10¢ to help defray the cost of the event.

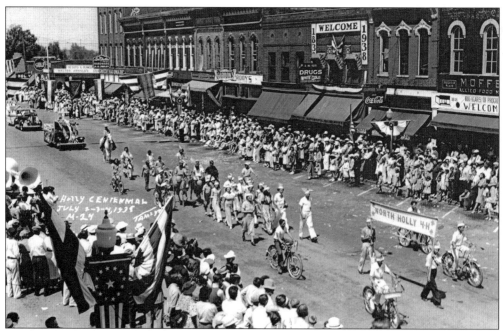

HOLLY CENTENNIAL PARADE. On Saturday, July 2, of the long weekend, there was a dedication of the American Legion Home preceded by a Drum & Bugle Corps Band. They dedicated Cyclone Park, followed by a parachute jump. Then there was a softball game at the ballpark and a historical pageant.

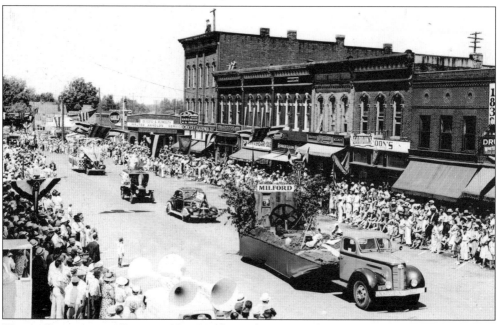

HOLLY CENTENNIAL PARADE. On Sunday, July 3, special services were held at all of the local churches and there was a reunion of all old Hollyites. Another ball game and a historical pageant were also held.

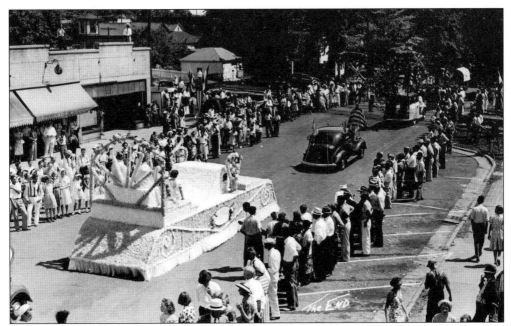

HOLLY CENTENNIAL PARADE. The big parade was on July 4, with five bands and many beautiful floats. The procession started on North Street, moved down Saginaw Street to Sherman and east to College Street, north to Maple Street, and west on Maple to Saginaw. The event followed with a fireworks display at Bevins Lake in the evening.

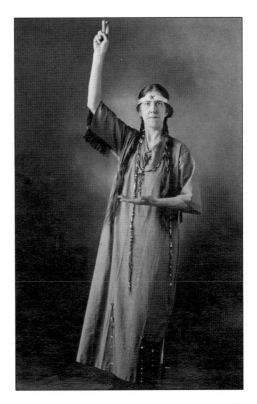

ELIZABETH HAMILTON, AS MONHATA, CENTENNIAL CELEBRATION 1938. According to Holly's centennial program, the historical pageant begins with the beginning of time and stories of the Native Americans. One legend of this area selected for the program was the story of the Green Lake medicine woman, Monhata. The waters of the lake reportedly had healing powers, and were visited by many young men. Ailing in spirit and seeking solace, neighboring chieftain Sashabaw visited the lake. He saw the lovely Monhata and lost his heart to her. In the performance, Sashabaw sings the "Indian Love Call" and Monhata replies with the song "The Land of the Sky Blue Water."

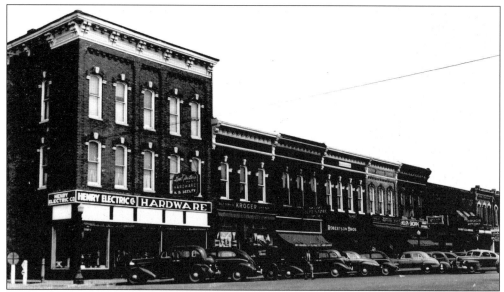

Corner of Maple and Saginaw, Looking South. Holly underwent many changes during the early 1940s. Businesses developed first along Broad Street and then along Saginaw Street, with Martha Street serving as a bridge between the two. This photo shows the changes in the many shops in downtown Holly, including Henry Electric, Kroger Grocery Store, and Robertson Brothers. The automobile styles have changed, as well.

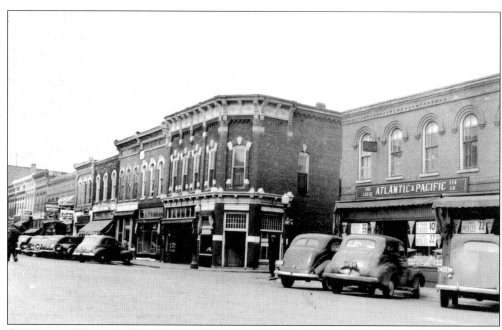

Corner of Martha Street and Saginaw Street, East Side. The Great Atlantic & Pacific Tea Company, otherwise known as the A&P, had a prominent spot on the corner. The time frame is early 1940s. (Photo courtesy James Hilty and Evelyn Raskin Hilty.)

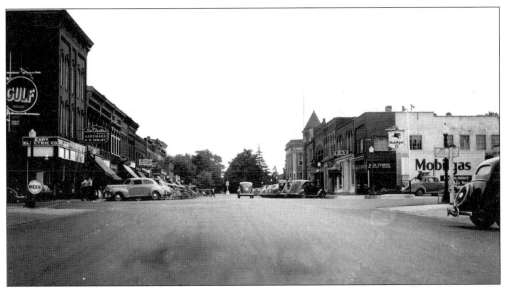

SAGINAW STREET, LOOKING SOUTH. There are gas stations on two of the four corners in the heart of town. (Photo courtesy of Don Simons.)

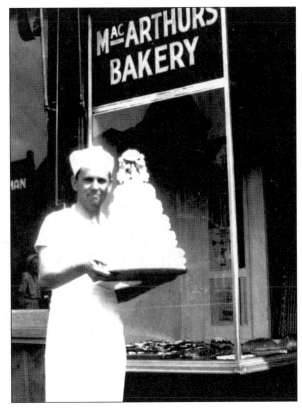

MACARTHUR'S BAKERY. As a young married couple, Gladys and Carl MacArthur left Flushing, Michigan, for Holly in 1938. "They bet all their dough on their future success in Holly . . . and dough it was, bread dough, cookie dough, pie dough . . . " wrote the *Goodfellow* newspaper. Pictured is Al Grasly with a wedding cake. (Photo courtesy of Carl MacArthur.)

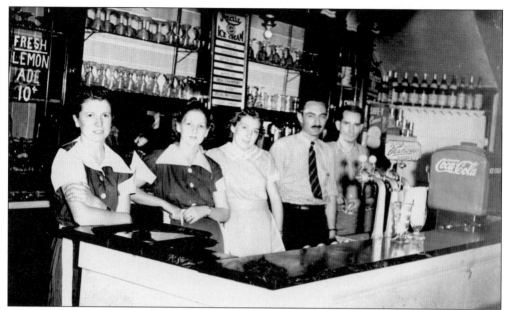

HOLLY'S SODA FOUNTAIN. This is Dyke's Soda Shop in the 1930s. Located in downtown Holly on Saginaw Street are, from left to right: Billie Taylor, Sally Carnegie Taylor, Rose Coleman Bezdisney, Donald Mackey (otherwise known as "Dyke"), and Charles Mackey. (Photo courtesy of Bruce Dryer.)

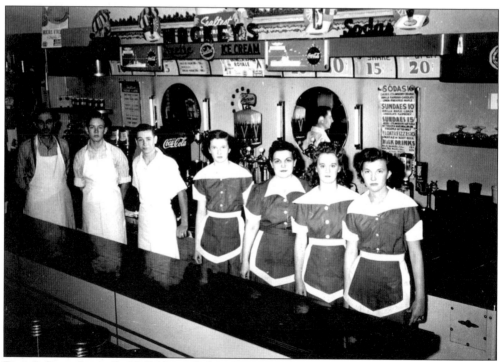

DYKE'S SODA SHOP. By 1943, the soda fountain had put on a new face. The staff included, from left: Dyke Mackey, Bruce Dryer, Harold Jones, Eleanor Keener Hill, Charlotte Nessman, Evelyn Hill Baker, and June Keener Montgomery. (Photo courtesy of Bruce Dryer.)

Four

EDUCATION

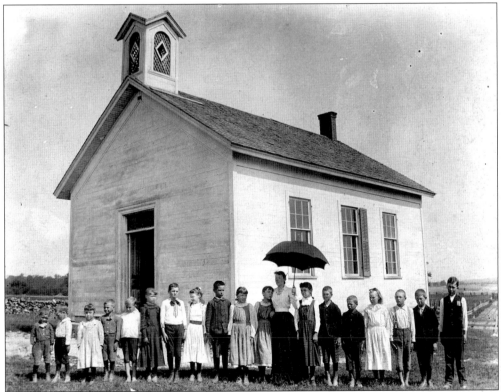

OLIVE BRANCH SCHOOL. Moses Smith came to Holly Township in 1835. He gave the name Olive Branch to the area where his house was located. It was on East Holly Road, from Falk Road, and encompassed Weber Road, Tucker Road, Warden Road, and Buckell Lake Road. It included a church, cemetery, and a school long before Holly Village existed.

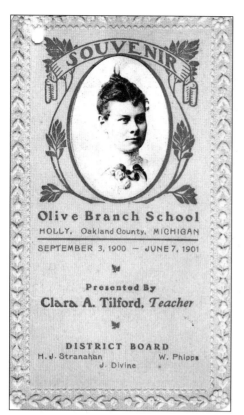

OLIVE BRANCH SCHOOL SOUVENIR PROGRAM. Clara A. Tilford, a teacher at Olive Branch School, printed this little souvenir to celebrate a year's worth of work. Dated September 3, 1900 to June 7, 1901, this would have been handed out as a program at the end of the school year. The paper was embossed and put together with a silk tassel. It also included a lovely photograph of the instructor.

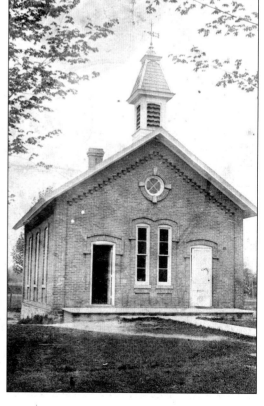

WARD SCHOOL. The one-story brick Ward School was located on the northwest corner of Saginaw and Sherman Streets. The school was built in 1876 at the cost of $1,000. In later years, it was used for first and second grades only. (Photo courtesy of David V. Tinder.)

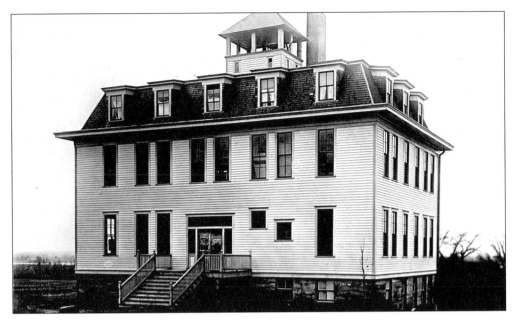

ADELPHIAN ACADEMY ADMINISTRATION BUILDING AND ACADEMY FACULTY HOME. The Seventh Day Adventists began meeting at Baird's Opera House in 1865. A site known as the Lacy Home, west of the village on 77 acres of land, was chosen for the group. The Adelphian Academy, established in 1905, was both a school and church organization. The Administration Building was built in 1907. It housed the chapel where Adventists from the village met for services with the academy staff and students until 1922. The church on Lake Street was built at this time. The faculty residence was built in 1911.

Since the school was residential, students were each required to bring a kerosene lamp. They also had to bring a mattress tick, which could be filled with straw and would serve as a bed. The school operated its own farm, dairy, culinary and dining room, bakery, laundry, print shop, and mill. The entire staff was fed from their own products and young people learned a trade. (Photos courtesy of James Hilty and Evelyn Raskin Hilty.)

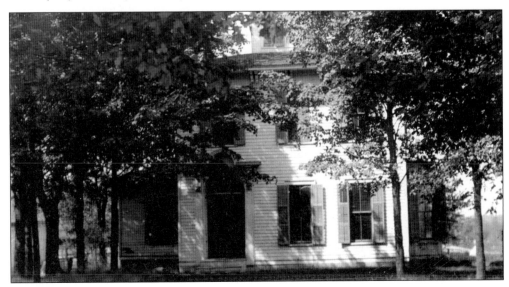

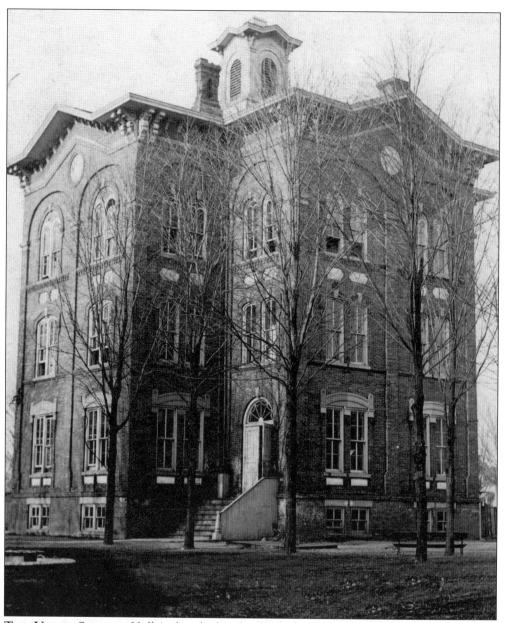

THE UNION SCHOOL. Holly's first high school was built in 1867 on College Street and completed in 1868. It was a grand three-story brick structure with a cupola at the very top and could be seen from the railroad depot. Since that time, the village has been the area's center of secondary learning. This unique building housed the high school on the top floor and the lower grades on the other two remaining floors. There were two classrooms on each floor, with two grades sharing a classroom. The Ward School was built on the corner of Saginaw and Sherman Streets in 1876 to provide additional grade school space.

Originally, the high school was heated by wood-burning stoves. During particularly cold days, school would have to be cancelled. Steam heat was not added until 1905. Since there was no public transportation, students walked, rode horseback, or rode in a buggy. If it was too far to travel, they boarded in town.

THE UNION SCHOOL, ANOTHER VIEW. From this photo, the two different entrances to the school are visible. In those days, girls and boys were separated until they entered class. The girls entered from a door toward the south side of the building, while boys used the entrance toward the north side. They were also not permitted to use the same playground. (Photo courtesy of Connie Davis.)

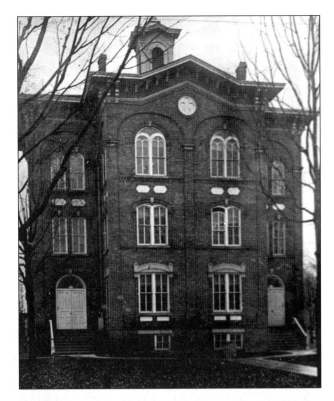

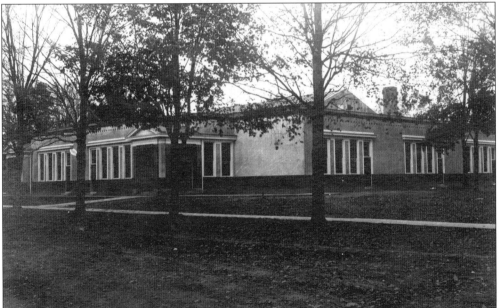

THE SECOND HIGH SCHOOL, C. 1917. The Union School was torn down in 1912, right after school let out for the summer. The bricks from the building were saved for use in the new structure. The cost of this project was approximately $30,000. Until the new high school was completed, students were taught at Baird's Opera House and several of the local churches. (Photo courtesy of James Hilty and Evelyn Raskin Hilty.)

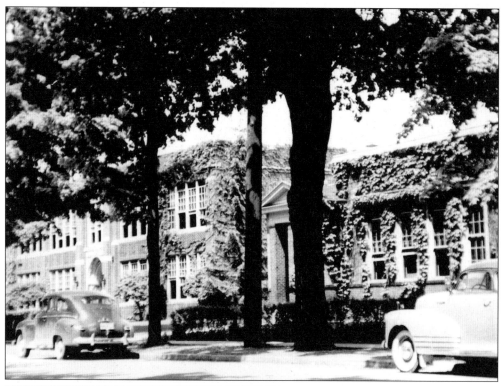

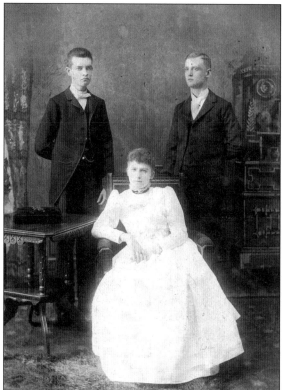

THE SECOND HIGH SCHOOL, C. 1926. By 1911, it had not been difficult to persuade the voters that the Union School was inadequate and had become a fire hazard. The planners went to the opposite extreme and selected a one-story design. Pressure from the North Central Educational Association compelled the school to take steps for further expansion. A two-story addition was added so the school could now offer commercial courses, homemaking, science, and a gymnasium. The school was named the Mabel Bensett School and is now called the Community Education Building.

CLASS OF 1890. Well into the 20th century, graduating high school classes in Holly often numbered under 20 students. In the front row is Metta Buzzell. In the back row are Ward Wickens (left) and Emery Humphrey (right).

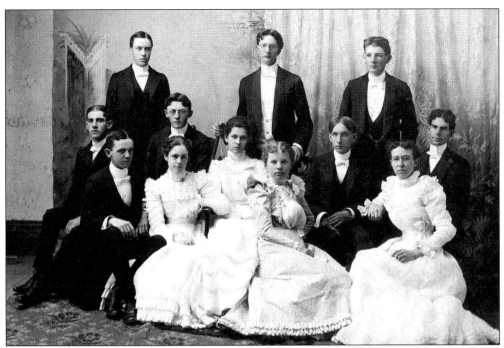

CLASS OF 1899. On the back of the photograph is the caption: "Girls, Blanche Joslin, Vera Lockwood, Agnes Robertson, and Gertrude Bigelow; Boys, George McGougal, Howard Alger, Lester Cross, Aden Manley, Clain Fullam, Allen, Mothersill, Lee Johnson, and Will Holdridge."

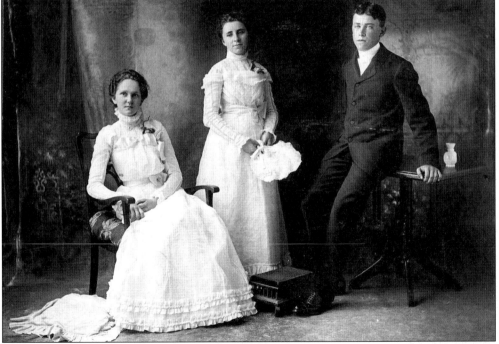

CLASS OF 1900. Graduation ceremonies were held in Baird's Opera House on Broad Street and admission was charged. From left to right are Maude Fagan, Clara Highfield, and Jesse Wright.

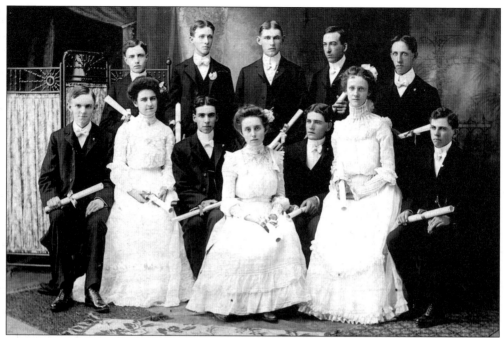

CLASS OF 1901. Pictured above are, from left to right: (front row) Homer Robbins, Mable Phipps, Frank Mitchell, Ethel Patterson, Richard Welch, Bessie Beach, and Walter Parker; (back row) Claud Bogart, King Beech, Ernest Bastian, Herbert Norris, and Charles Streeter.

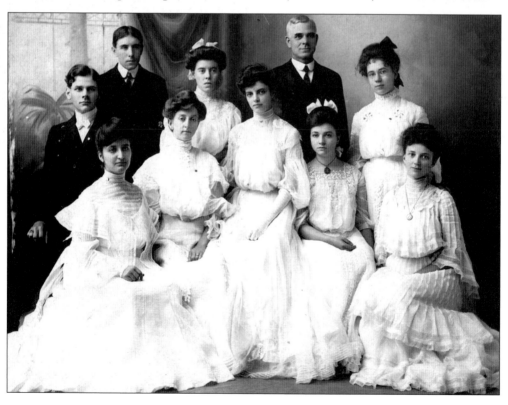

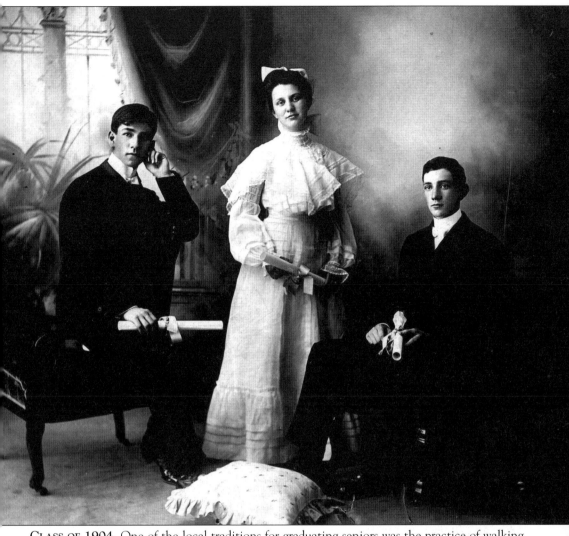

CLASS OF 1904. One of the local traditions for graduating seniors was the practice of walking out on the last day of classes. The entire student body, faculty, and townspeople would gather on the lawn of the school and watch the senior class walk out of the school for the last time.

In 1905, there were approximately 428 students attending the Union School. By the next year, the population had increased to 600 students. The high school faculty was small. The superintendent and principal taught classes as well as ran the school. There was a teacher for English and Math, but the curriculum was limited. It required 16 units of credit for graduation. In 1910 the superintendent earned an annual salary of $810. The teachers made between $32.40 and $50 a month.

The graduating students of 1904 were Varnum Jones (left), Mary Clark (center), and Mark Mothersill (right).

Opposite: **CLASS OF 1903.** Pictured are, from left to right: (front row) Edith Marks, Etta Bowman, Maude Eastwood, Laura Wright, and Goldie Halstead; (back row) Fred Bigelow, Will Gidley, Grace Brodie, Superintendent S.O. Wood, and Nellie McKinney.

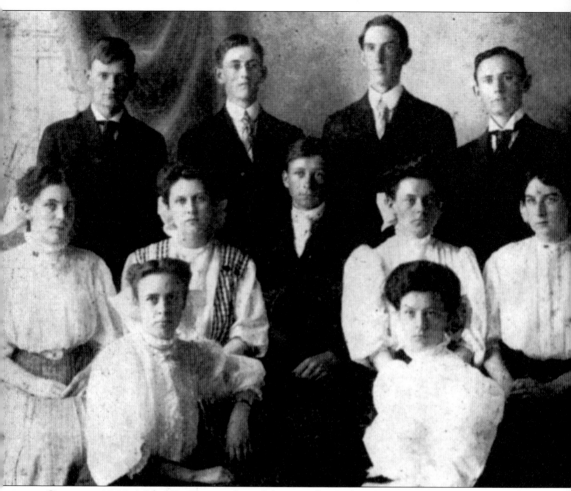

CLASS OF 1908. Mabel Bensett graduated from Holly High School in 1908. She spent a short time teaching in the rural schools before coming to Holly, where she spent 46 consecutive years at one school. She took one year to attend Michigan State Normal College in Ypsilanti, where she received her B.S. in 1925. Beginning with the sixth and seventh grades, promotions followed consistently as she served in many capacities. Each promotion was a forward step; she first became principal of the Holly Junior High, and then principal of Holly High School. Pictured here are, from left to right: (front row) Mabel Summerville and Zeta Jarrett; (middle row) Mabel Bensett, Shirley Smith, Peter Fagan, Zoe Jarrett, and Eva Gordon; (back row) Arthur Andrews, Elmore Sutton, Dave Patterson, and Herman McLellan.

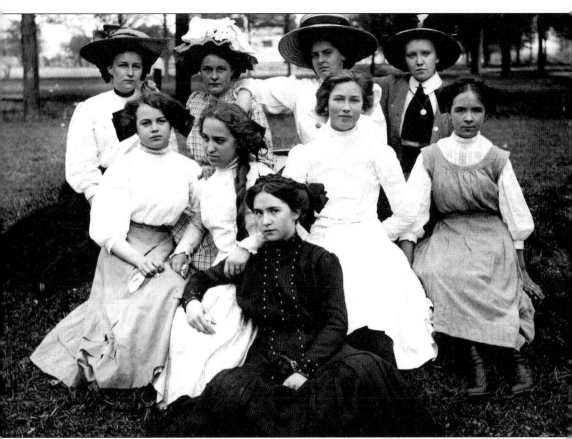

EIGHTH GRADE GIRLS, 1910. These proper ladies had a more informal portrait taken outside. As the graduating eighth grade girls, they would then go on to high school classes. Their ages ranged between 13 and 15 years old. Grades were established according to the student's proficiency. In the front row is Ruth Marsh, who grew up to be a trained nurse, and was never married. Pictured in the middle row are, from left to right: Velma Curtis, Sylvia Martin Tubbs, Mary G. Coville Elliott, and Florence Cameron Kerton. In the back row are, from left: Hopey Hoxworth, Marsh Sorsensen, Louisa Hellman Johnson, Helen Pearson, and Nada Henning Mitchell. There was additional information on the back of the photograph noting that Florence was the youngest, followed by May. Both Hopey and Nada were born in 1893, while Louisa and Ruth were born in 1895.

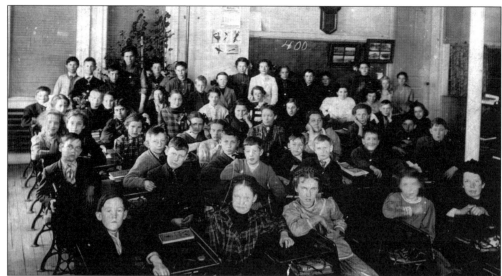

SIXTH AND SEVENTH GRADES, 1911. This is an interior of the Union School just before it was torn down. There were two grades to a classroom.

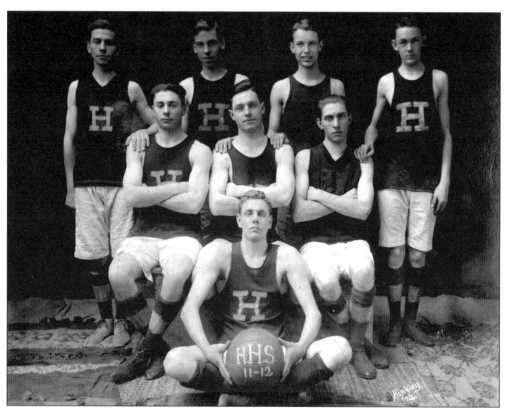

HOLLY HIGH SCHOOL BASKETBALL TEAM, 1911–1912. At this time, the Union School was scheduled to be torn down and a new high school was to be constructed. Since there were no gym facilities available at the old school, sports teams played on the third floor of Baird's Opera House on Broad Street. The photograph was taken in a studio with carpet on the floor.

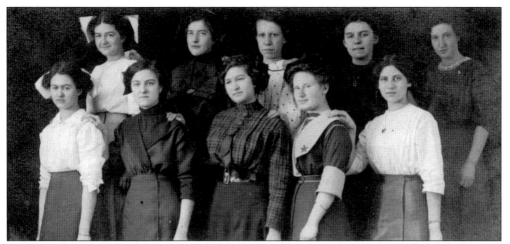

JUNIOR GIRLS, 1912. Pictured here are, from left to right: (front row) Verna Chaffee, Ella Hines, Jennie Scott, Marion Haddon, and Flossie Taylor; (back row) Daisy Hall, Rotha Gibbes, Beatrice Henning, Eunice Devine, and Dolly Vout.

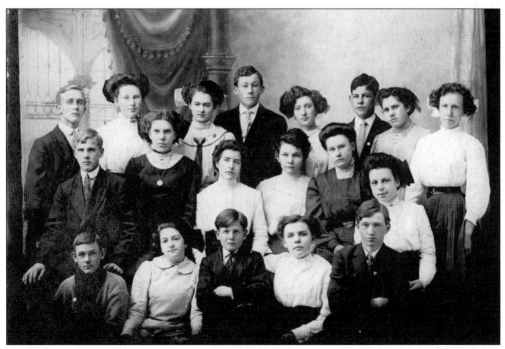

ELEVENTH GRADE, 1912. Pictured from left to right are as follows: (front row) Burton Daugherty, Daisy Hall, George Cornell, Eunice Devine, and Kellon Mackey; (middle row) Fred Deno, Joyce Jarrett, Rotha Gibbs, Etta Perry, Irma Mills, and unidentified; (back row) Forest Beebe, Marion Haddon, Vern Chaffee, Henry Seeley, Dolly Vout, Paul Lockwood, Daisy Scott, and Beatrice Henning.

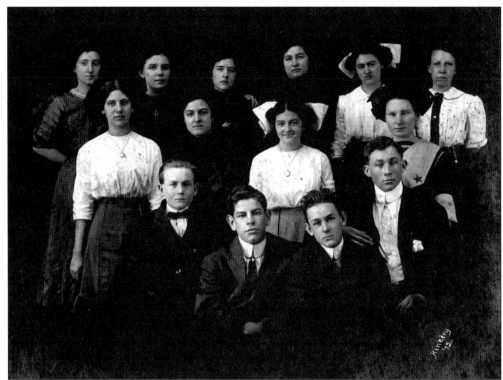

CLASS OF 1912. This was the last senior graduating class from the Union School. During the fall of 1912 and the winter of 1913, classes were held on the second and third floors of Baird's Opera House. After the 1913 Easter vacation, the new high school building was ready.

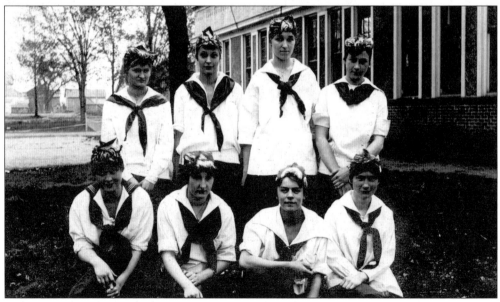

CLASS OF 1916. This photograph of the senior girls in their gym uniforms was taken in front of the new high school. The names listed are Verna Bradley, Marion Tharett, Maude Mills, Andre Bird, Ruth Chaffee Beckley, Dorothy Dunlap, Gene McBratney, and Martell Barnett.

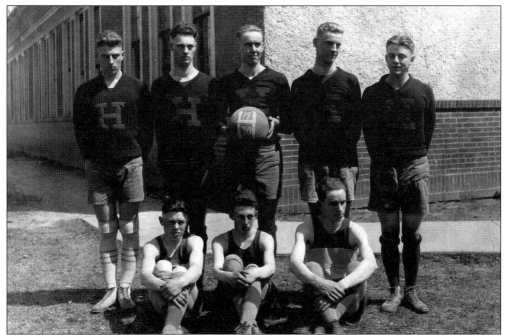

HOLLY HIGH SCHOOL BASKETBALL, 1919–1920. Pictured are, from left: (front row) Tiber Thompson, Hugh Wilkinson, Howard Green; (back row) Cliff Povenz, John Lamb, Captain Tom Hadley, Dick Love, and Jim Clarke.

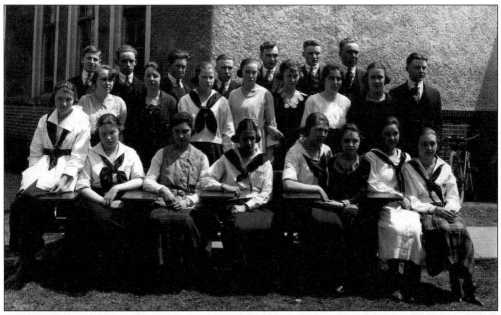

CLASS OF 1920. Pictured from left are as follows: (front row) Ruth Long, Norma Green, Arlene King, Thelma Beatty, Lucille Shubert, Geraldeen Smith, Arlene Cook, Frances Rusche; (middle row) Geneva Hubele, Margaret Benson, Esther Munger, Gladys Hitchcock, Josephine Arnold, Mabel Bensett, teacher, and Josephine Based; (back row) Max Krasnik, Howard Green, Buck Smithingill, Gordon Munger, Grant McNulty, Stewart Patterson, Tom Hadley, and Jim Clark.

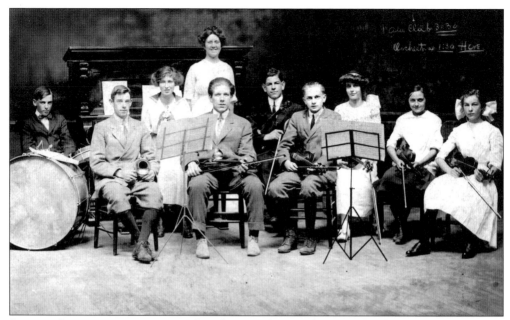

SCHOOL ORCHESTRA, C. 1920S. This photograph was taken in school with the note on the blackboard that reads, "The orchestra meets here at 1:30." Pictured from left to right are Wilson Curtis, Kirby Milleur, May Coville, Harold Kenyon, Paul Lockwood, Maurice Winglemire, Dorothy Dunlop, Lina Atherton, and Irene Summerville. The teacher is Helen S. Wood.

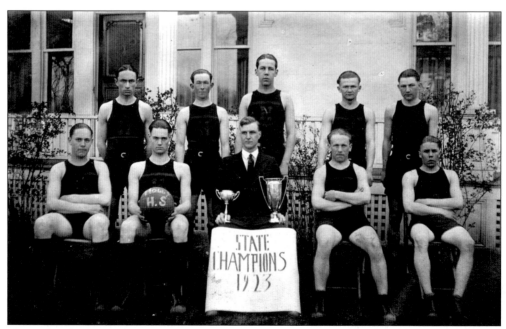

HOLLY HIGH SCHOOL BASKETBALL STATE CHAMPIONS, 1923. Team members pictured here are, from left to right: (front row) John Waldo, John Lamb, Russell Van Avery, coach, Brian Beatty, and Elias Hartz; (back row) Donald Mackey, Fred Disbrow, Dick Carter, Ferdinand Schultz, and David Donaldson.

Five
RESIDENTIAL AREAS

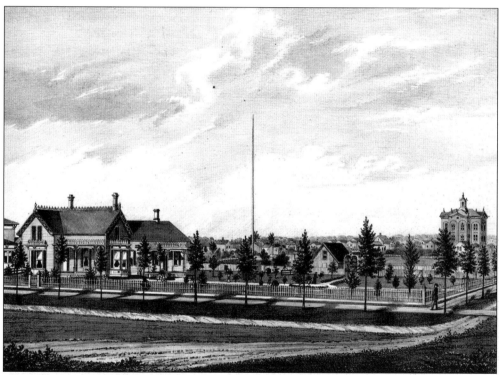

RICHARD HOUGHIN RESIDENCE. This etching was taken out of an early *Oakland County Register*. The home was located on the corner of Washington and Baird. The asymmetrical building was constructed in the Victorian era, with details representing both Gothic Revival and Queen Anne styles. The Union School is shown on the right side of the picture. (Courtesy of James Hilty and Evelyn Raskin Hilty.)

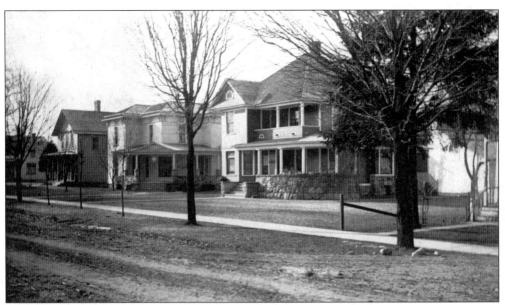

308, 306, 304, AND 302 SOUTH SAGINAW STREET. From left to right are the two homes that were owned by the Hadley family, followed by the McDonald family home and the Peter Jacobs home. The Jacobs home is no longer there, having been replaced by a street following along the railroad tracks.

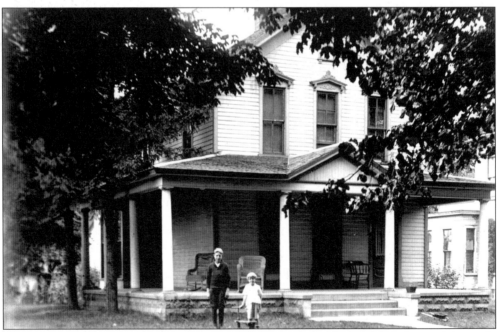

308 SOUTH SAGINAW STREET, 1868. This home is considered a modified Queen Anne-style house. The large porch had been altered before this picture was taken. Former owners include the Hadley family, who also lived next door. The younger generation of Hadleys would reside here first. The parlor was segregated from the rest of the home, and saved for Sunday visitors and special occasions. (Photo courtesy of Michael S. and Lisa Clemons.)

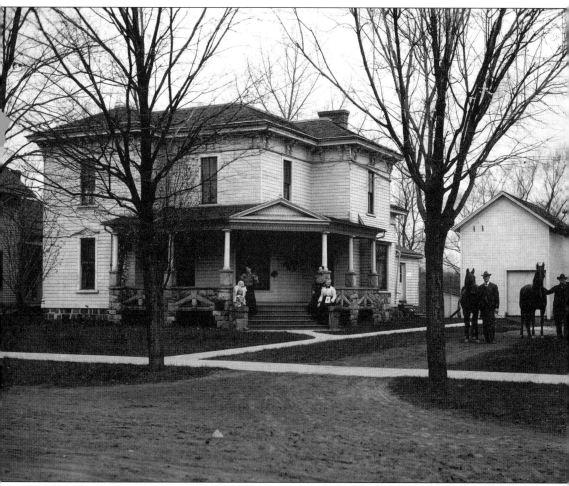

306 SOUTH SAGINAW STREET. The Hadley House was built in 1873 and was first occupied by Dr. Daniel D. Bartholomew. He lived and practiced medicine here until the early 1900s. In 1902, Dr. Barthomew bought Holly's first horseless carriage, a Brush runabout with a folded buggy top, one seat, a patent leather dash board and whipped socket, a steering rod, and wooden spoke hard-rubber-tired wheels.

The next owner of the home was Darwin Darius Hadley, who died in 1920. His widow lived here until her death in her 90s. Then her son, Clyde, resided here until his death. Tom and Arlene Hadley were the last owners of the home. Tom was a well-known architectural engineer, inventor, and poet. He and his wife, Arlene, used film to capture the beauty of nature. He was the host of several programs on wildlife, including "Nature Trails" which appeared on WWJ-TV in Detroit during the 1950s.

After Tom died, Arlene lived here alone until 1986, when she sold the home to the Holly Historical Society. The organization had outgrown the Patterson House on Maple Street. The Hadley House is now a museum, decorated in the interior in the Victorian style, featuring furniture and accessories popular from 1860 until 1900. The home is original with the exception of one wall in the kitchen, which has a new sink and counter, and the wallpaper in three rooms, which has been replaced.

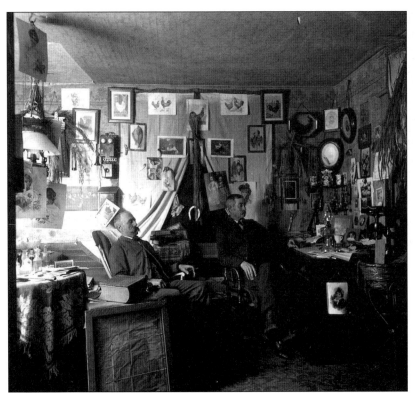

This is a 1903 interior image of the home of E.D. Bussey on South Saginaw Street. Mr. Bussey wrote, describing his retreat, "This picture shows my office room—what is sometimes called a man's den. But I do not like the later name."

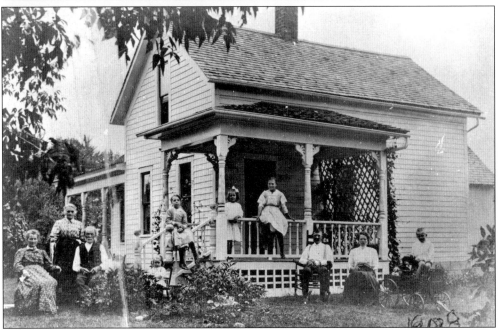

105 LAKE STREET. Vera Cook Husted is shown on the railing of her home in 1908. Vera grew up to have quite a reputation as local historian, since the Cook family has lived in the Holly area since 1869. She was a long-time resident, working as an artist, sign painter, and architect, all while collecting historical data for posterity. (Photo courtesy of Don Winglemire.)

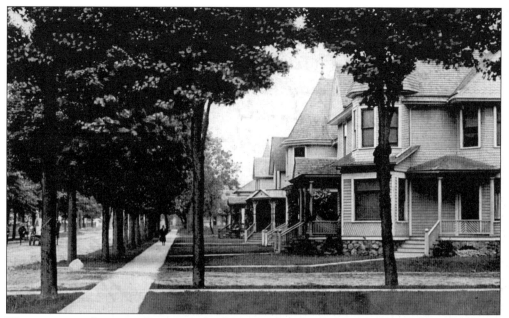

WASHINGTON AVENUE, LOOKING SOUTH. The house on the corner was built by Moses Downing in 1894, in the Victorian style. It has a beautiful fireplace in the centrally-located parlor along with two staircases. In the early 1900s, Dr. Felshaw lived and practiced out of the house. There are two entrances; one was used for company and the other for business.

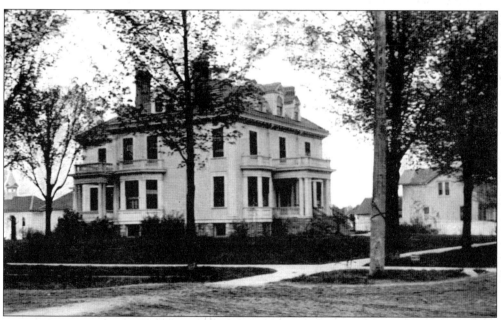

212 COLLEGE STREET. James Bailey, of the famous Barnum & Bailey Circus, built this beautiful mansion for his brother, Edward McGinnis, in 1903. The elegant home is graced with beautiful carved woodwork and seven fireplaces. Occasionally, circus animals were housed or tethered near the carriage house. The two brothers were known locally for their business ventures, raising fighting game cocks and race horses.

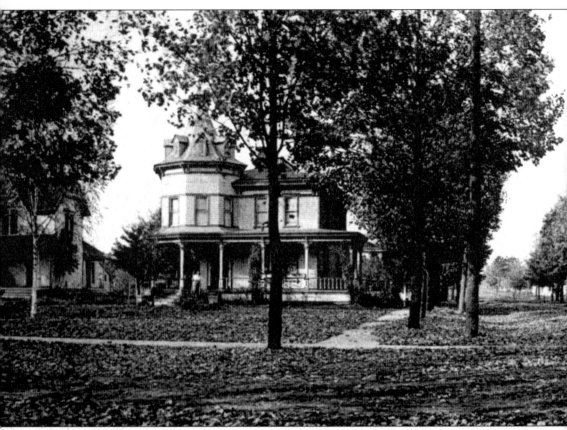

MAPLE STREET PANORAMA, LOOKING LEFT. James B. Simonson was the original farmer and landowner of this neighborhood. It was prime property because of the lake location, the lake bearing his name and located behind these homes.

John M. Baird built the grand house in the center of the photograph. In 1867, Mr. Baird came to Michigan to sell nursery stock from New York. He invested in five acres of land in Holly Village and platted it. The business venture was so successful and he enjoyed the community so much that John decided to settle in Holly with his new bride. He bought and platted more land, about 53 acres, on which many of the finest homes in town were built. This included the site of the old high school on College Street.

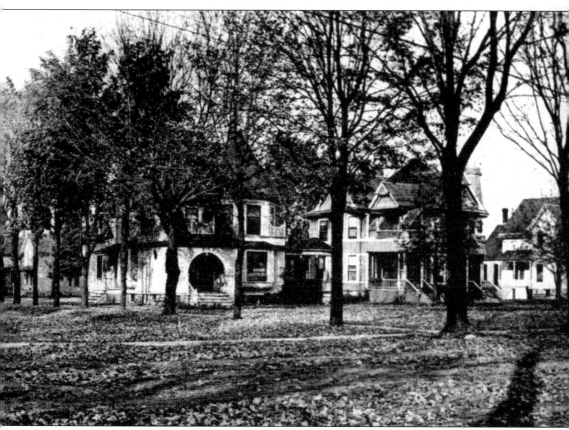

MAPLE STREET PANORAMA, LOOKING RIGHT. The maple trees that furnished the foliage for which Holly is noted were planted by William "Billy" Green, a lifetime resident of Holly. For 60 years, Green lived in a house on Maple Street, shaded by maples he had planted in his youth. He is known to have enjoyed a daily swim in Simonson Lake, which was located behind his home, until he was in his 90s.

Most of the young maples came from the farm of his brother, Morris, north of Holly. There was a fine sugar bush in a place where the farm animals were not allowed to trample down the saplings. One spring, he took out 900 of those saplings and delivered them to Holly, Fenton, Clarkston, Waterford, and Pontiac. He began the practice of cutting ice from the lake, and it grew into a thriving business. Refrigeration consisted of ice in a metal-lined wood box.

Green said that he gained his knowledge of tree life from his very first job as a small boy. He helped a Chicago man take small trees out of the woods to replant elsewhere. Green was paid $5 and given a Newfoundland dog.

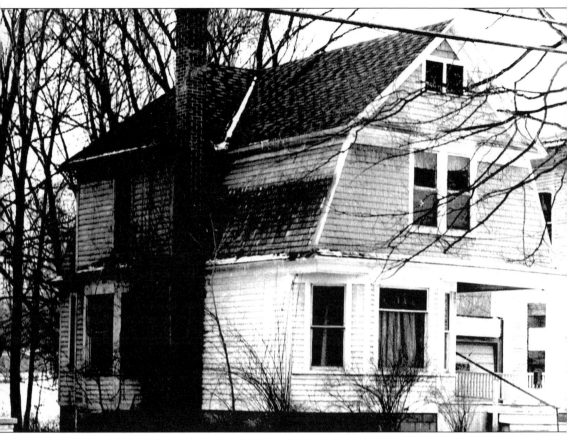

502 East Maple Street. Frederick Patterson built this house for his bride, Eliza Jones, in 1905. The Dutch Colonial design is rare in Michigan and throughout the United States. After America's centennial anniversary, there was a revival of colonial architecture. With popular interest still resting heavily on elaborate Victorian styles, this design was the antithesis: simple and cozy. Interior spaces were small—the middle class favored this. The unusual roofline is called a sloping gambrel and is characteristic of this style. This type of building always has two stories, sometimes with dormers. Wooden parapets may have projected above the roof level.

Both of the Patterson children were born at the residence, George in 1906, and Elizabeth in 1908. Fred and Eliza owned and operated the *Holly Advertiser* newspaper for forty years. The Holly Historical Society, formerly known as the Northwest Oakland County Historical Society, eventually bought the house from the family. Here, the society created the first museum of its kind in Holly. The building has since returned to private ownership.

501 East Maple. The C.P. Bissell Home, *c.* 1900, is located on the northeast corner of Maple and Clarence Street. Mr. Bissell was a traveling salesman for approximately 40 years. He was president of the Michigan Manufacturing and Lumber Company and traveled throughout North America, from Maine to Oregon and from Canada to Cuba.

The interior shown below is from an original photograph taken inside the Bissell home during the Victorian era. The floors are oak, left bare with large area rugs on top. The furniture is not large, but it is fussy, with lots of turned wood. The walls and ceiling are both wallpapered, and there is plenty of architectural trim, and heavy drapery to close off the rooms. The parlor was generally separated from the rest of the house, and used only for special occasions, especially holidays and funerals.

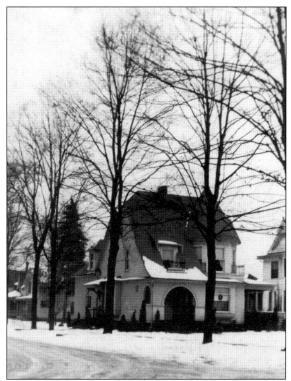

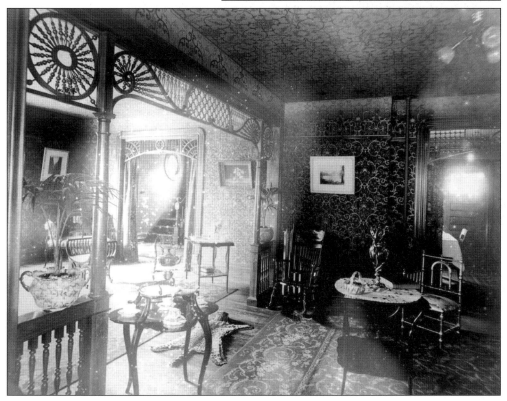

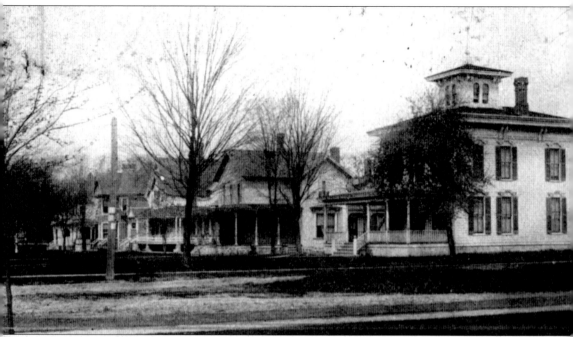

511 East Maple. George Pomeroy built this house in 1870, located on the corner of Lake Street. He was an agent for Michigan's Governor Crapo, assigned to assist in bringing the railroad to Holly. In 1876, Captain Elliot, who fought in the Civil War, purchased the home. His one child, a daughter named Marian, lived there from 1900 until 1983. Because she lived there for such a long time, Marian spent a lot of time "modernizing" the old house. She eventually dismantled the fireplaces and replaced the old-fashioned bay windows with picture windows.

The structure is considered to be in the Italianate style, complete with a large cupola on the upper story. The cupola caught fire in 1910, when the house next door burned down. Captain Elliot replaced it with a Widow's Walk. He also moved and shortened the staircase, which had started on the first floor and went up to the attic. (Photo courtesy of Vincent and Malinda Simon.)

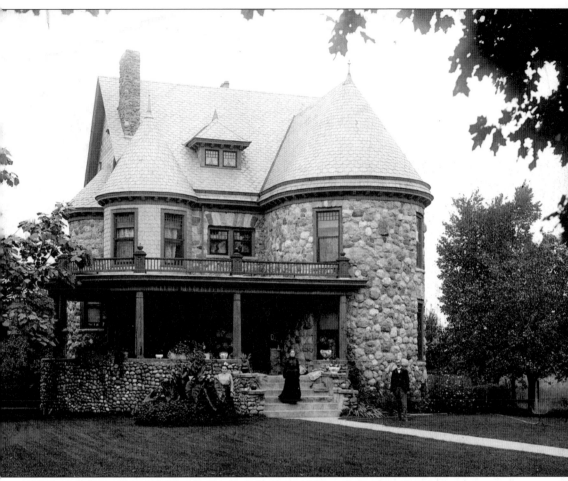

701 East Maple Street. This home dates back to 1893, a time when the closer you were to Saginaw Street and the business area, the better. Mr. C.F. Collier had the house built entirely from fieldstones drawn from various farms near Holly. The roof and gables were built with slate from Vermont. The ceilings on the first floor are nine-and-one-half feet high and every room is finished in oak, except the hall and parlor, which are finished in cherry.

When built, the house was lighted throughout with electric lights instead of gas. A large pantry was constructed with a china closet, with a chest and built-in drawers for table linens. There was a dumbwaiter running from the cellar to the second floor. It served the laundry, kitchen, and second-floor back hallway. The bathroom was complete with all the modern conveniences, including a porcelain-lined bathtub. In the 1900 photograph are then-current resident Belle Maybee Jones (left), her mother, Jesse Maybee (center), and James R. Jones (right).

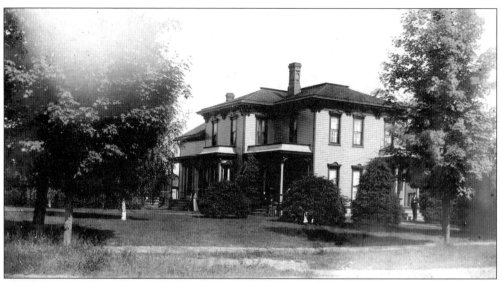

201 COLLEGE. Another example of Victorian Italianate architecture, this home has a simple hip roof with large eave brackets, inspired by rambling Italian farmhouses. Sprawled on a large lot with plenty of narrow, tall, pedimented windows, the construction was a sign of prosperity. This style was common in the growing towns of the Midwest between 1850 and 1880.

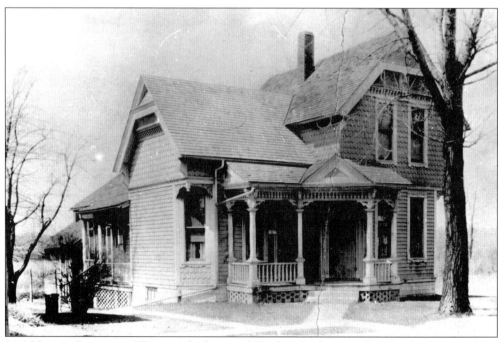

307 NORTH SAGINAW. This was the home of "Packy" Anderson, who was the Justice of the Peace. He was related to the Cook family and would gather with them for Thanksgiving. They ate in the basement and had the perimeters of the walls decorated with turkey wishbones from previous years. (Photo courtesy of Don Winglemire.)

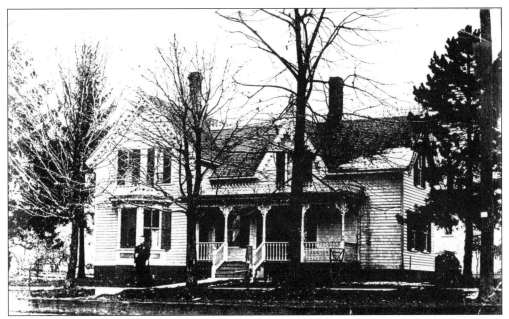

400 North Saginaw. This Victorian home was located on the corner of Elm and Saginaw Streets. It was the home of the Robert and Mary Ann Haddon family. The photograph was taken in 1920 and the structure housed 11 children. Many of the Haddon's 27 grandchildren visited here. (Photo courtesy of Lois Caryl.)

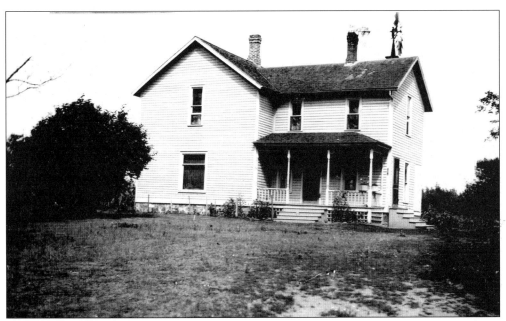

12239 North Holly Road. This farmhouse was built between 1870 and 1875. It is a Centennial Farm, which began in a log cabin across the street. The fourth generation of Mitchells now live there and operate a cattle farm at that location. (Photo courtesy of L.P. and Virginia Mitchell.)

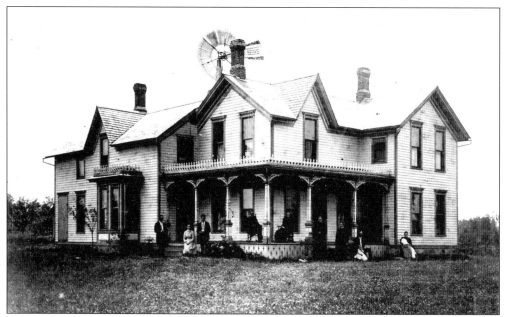

3404 Mitchell Road. Built between 1885 and 1890, this farmhouse was built in the Victorian style called Queen Anne, with a large porch that could be used on a warm sunny day. At one time, the house was heated by wood stoves, which were also used for cooking. The stoves were located in the dining room, living room, and parlor. The oak woodwork was harvested from trees on the farm. The windmill pumped water for the family as well as the livestock. Water was stored in a concrete tank. (Photo courtesy of Glen and Candace Mitchell.)

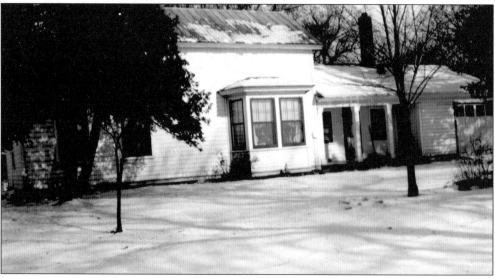

5105 Lahring Road. John Lahring came from Germany in 1838 and lived in a log cabin about 100 feet east of the existing home on Gravel Lake. He was a farmer all of his life and started with 40 acres, eventually owning 200 acres. The family has the original Land Grant, signed by President Millard Fillmore. Built from 1845 to 1850, the building has a metal roof, which replaced the original wood shingles. The well was dug by hand. The names of roads were designated after the original farm owners. (Photo courtesy of Roy Lahring.)

Six
RELIGIOUS LIFE

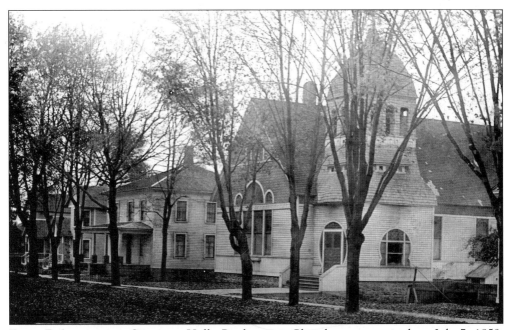

FIRST PRESBYTERIAN CHURCH. Holly Presbyterian Church was organized on July 7, 1859. There were eight charter members. The Reverend George Winter, an itinerant preacher from Independence (Sashabaw Plains), Michigan, was the pastor. The church met in the old schoolhouse on South Saginaw, and also in the new Methodist Church.

The growing Holly Presbyterian Church was given a lot on Maple Street by J.B. Simonson, near the lake that bears his name. Early in 1861, ground was broken for a building 32 feet by 52 feet. By Christmas, it was finished, furnished, and free of debt for the modest sum of $2,200. (Photo courtesy of James Hilty and Evelyn Raskin Hilty.)

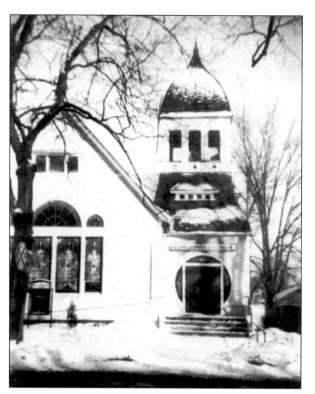

SKETCH OF FIRST PRESBYTERIAN CHURCH. In 1862, the Presbyterians presented Holly with its first "church going bell." The church later burned down in 1889. Many furnishings and records were saved. "The church burned out about noon, it being the day of the annual sleigh ride for the Sabbath School. Weather being zero all day . . . cause of the fire was the improper manner in which the thimble was bricked into the chimney." Another building was constructed on the spot within 246 days. This 1890 sanctuary is still in use today.

HOLLY BAPTIST CHURCH. In 1858, a Baptist congregation moved to Holly and held services in the old schoolhouse on Saginaw Street, under the leadership of Reverend H. Stowitts. In 1862, a frame church was built up the street at 400 South Saginaw. A Sunday school was organized in 1863 with James E. Church as the first superintendent. Calvin Bussey donated the site for the church.

Extensive repairs were made in the church in 1918 and 1919, and then in 1925, a fire, caused by an overheated furnace, damaged the building. There was extensive damage, but it was rebuilt. This building is still in use today by another congregation. (Photo courtesy of James Hilty and Evelyn Raskin Hilty.)

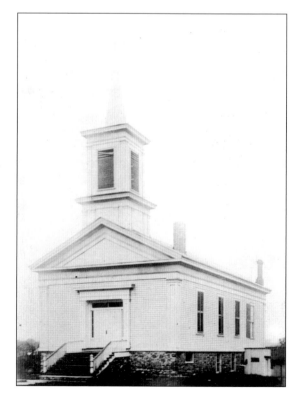

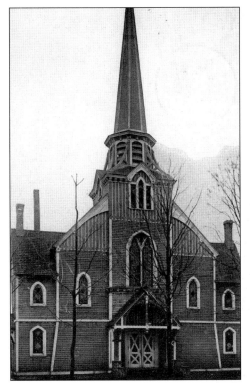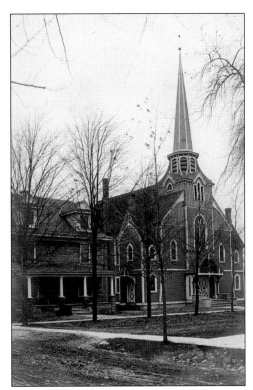

M.E. CHURCH AND PARSONAGE. Methodism came to Holly in 1840 in the neighborhood of Olive Branch. By 1856, Methodists moved to the Village of Holly. In 1857, a congregation was established and by 1859 there were 45 members.

Ira Alger, a local physician and pioneer, donated the land for the church. At a cost of $3,000, a structure was erected at the corner of John and Martha Streets. A parsonage was added later. The church was dedicated in 1859. Older residents recall that the outer walls were the same as at present, with high ceilings so characteristic of early church architecture. A second floor was laid midway, which provided ample Sunday school rooms below, as well as a kitchen. For a time, the Methodist and Episcopalian congregations met in this building.

In the fall of 1870, lightning splintered the tall spire. When the spire was repaired, the 1,022-pound bell was hoisted into place. The bell first rang out in January 1, 1871. The bell is still ringing today at the new church location. (Photos courtesy of James Hilty and Evelyn Raskin Hilty.)

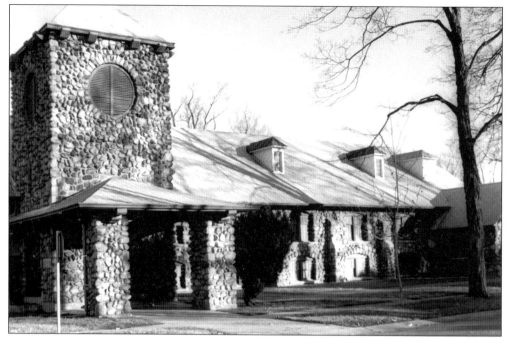

ST. RITA'S CATHOLIC CHURCH, 1927. Bishop Gallagher of Detroit and Mr. S. Pheney purchased the home of Clyde and Mabel Seeley, located on the corner of John and Maple Streets, in 1919. The interior was converted into a church and the women of the parish held a dinner to welcome home the veterans of the First World War.

Father M. Walsh began construction of the new stone church in the spring of 1921. The stones were gathered and hauled by horse and wagon from neighboring farm fields. By 1927, the outer building was completed, with the interior waiting until 1950.

If you think back on the history of this church, and what it took for them to get where they are today, the name St. Rita is very fitting. "The Saint of the Impossible made it possible for the parish to believe in a cause more worthy than their own, a cause to bring their parish into the community."

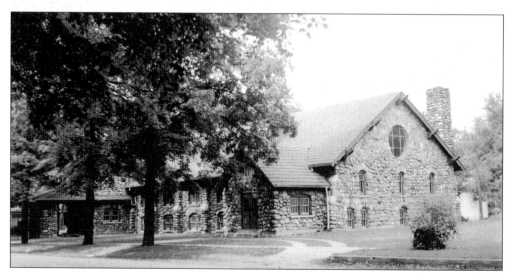

Seven
DAILY LIFE

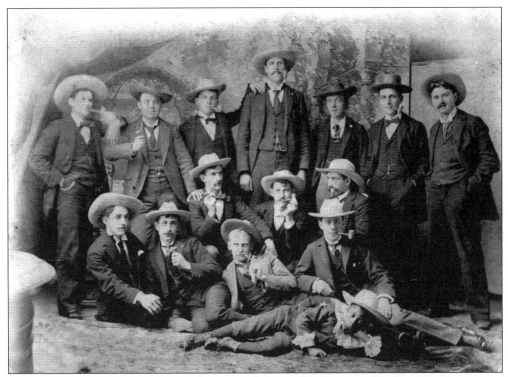

HOLLY MEN'S CLUB, 1898. Pictured are, from left to right: (front row) Emery Humphrey, John Alger, and Arthur Smith Younger; (middle row) James Barkham, John Plumb, Alt Macomber, Dick Reaume, and Dick Bensett; (back row) Frank M. Haddon, Dan Robertson, L.A. Meay Felshaw, Dr. Thomas McDonald, Tommy (John Alger's tailor), and Charles Felshaw.

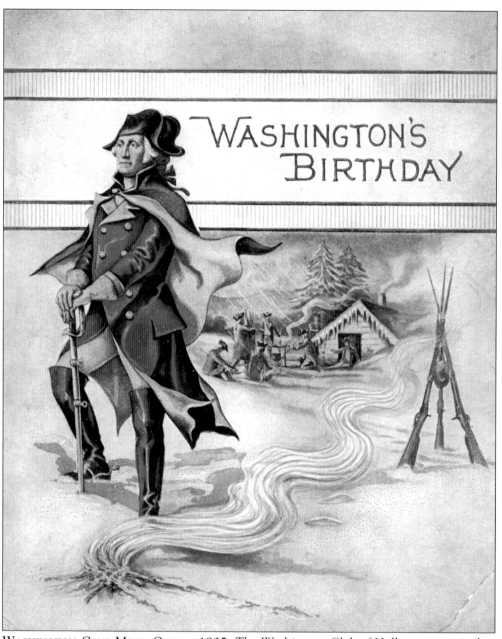

WASHINGTON CLUB MENU COVER, 1905. The Washington Club of Holly was organized in 1893 in the home of Mr. and Mrs. R.K. Divine for the purpose of celebrating Washington's Birthday each year. Also, they wanted to keep alive a love of American ideals and traditions. The club has never missed its yearly meeting since its organization, and some of Holly's most prominent citizens are among its officers.

For many years club members met at Baird's Opera House on Broad Street for their business session in the morning, and then adjourned to the Hirst Hotel, now the Holly Hotel, for dinner and a program. When the membership grew too large to be accommodated by the hotel, the banquets were held in the Presbyterian or Methodist Church dining rooms. The club has always been interdenominational and non-political.

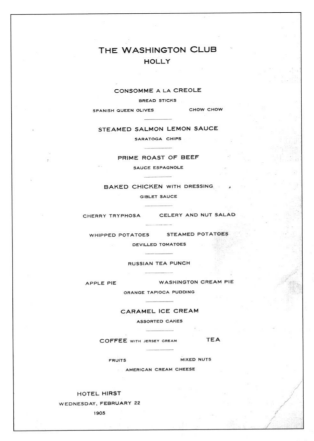

THE WASHINGTON CLUB
HOLLY

CONSOMME A LA CREOLE
BREAD STICKS
SPANISH QUEEN OLIVES   CHOW CHOW

STEAMED SALMON LEMON SAUCE
SARATOGA CHIPS

PRIME ROAST OF BEEF
SAUCE ESPAGNOLE

BAKED CHICKEN WITH DRESSING
GIBLET SAUCE

CHERRY TRYPHOSA   CELERY AND NUT SALAD

WHIPPED POTATOES   STEAMED POTATOES
DEVILLED TOMATOES

RUSSIAN TEA PUNCH

APPLE PIE   WASHINGTON CREAM PIE
ORANGE TAPIOCA PUDDING

CARAMEL ICE CREAM
ASSORTED CAKES

COFFEE WITH JERSEY CREAM   TEA

FRUITS   MIXED NUTS
AMERICAN CREAM CHEESE

HOTEL HIRST
WEDNESDAY, FEBRUARY 22
1905

WASHINGTON CLUB MENU, 1905. Included in Holly's Centennial Celebration Program in 1938 was a section celebrating the Washington Club. A special poem was written and presented:

Unique in plan and fine in its ideals
The Holly Washington Club perpetuates the name
And works of Washington, the man
Who brought America the most in honor and in fame.

Since 1893 this patriotic band
Has celebrated year by year his natal day
With song and speech and banquet gay
And pledged to spread his honor through the land.

A solemn oath was given everyone
Who joined this energetic club, for he must be
American in thought, and word and deed
Nor tolerate a red flag brought across the sea.

In 1932, this club took part
With others in the land to celebrate
The two hundredth birthday of our "First American"
The one whom history will know as "George, the Great."

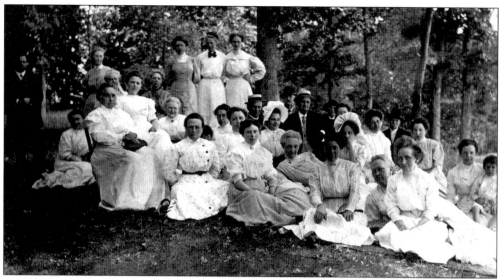

THE MONDAY CLUB PICNIC, JULY 13, 1910. The Monday Club was started on January 6, 1902. The areas through which the women worked, besides literary study, were literature and town improvement, municipal and legal, education, and art. The motto was "no nation is greater than its women." They met at the Hotel Norton at this time. The *Holly Herald* of June 13, 1908 reported: "We endeavor to carry out the County Federation's slogan, 'Leave the world a more beautiful place than you found it.'"

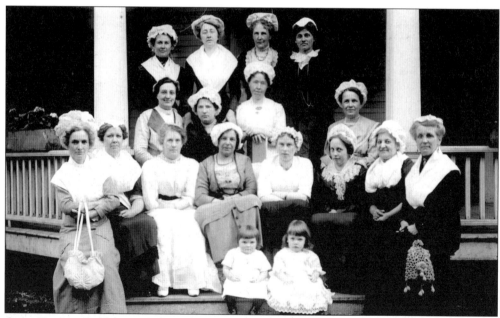

OPEN DAY OF THE MONDAY CLUB, MAY 7, 1918. Open Day of the Monday Club was held at the home of Mrs. Arthur Hadley. In foreground are a child of Mrs. Hinkley (left) and a child of Mrs. Waters (right). Pictured are, from left to right: (front row) Mrs. Meacham, Mrs. Seeley, Mrs. Skinner, Mrs. McDonegal, Mrs. Hinkley, Mrs. Waters, Mrs. Marko, and Mrs. Hovey; (middle row) Mrs. Smith, Mrs. Haas, Mrs. Lyman, and Mrs. Baird; (back row) Mrs. Westfall, Mrs. Lockwood, Mrs. Hadley, and Mrs. Andrews.

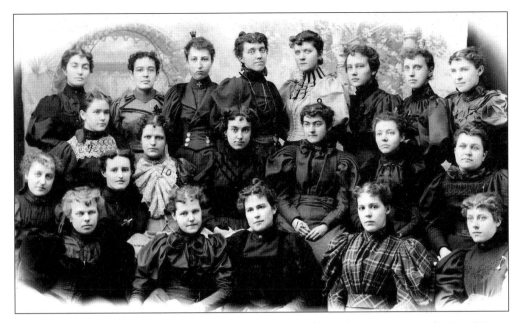

THE ELITE CLUB AND THE HOLLY WOMEN'S CLUB. In the early years, women had to do a lot of housework by hand, in addition to raising children, but they still joined organizations for social reasons as well as for community service. They found time to dress up, but also had a little fun with the girls with a casual picnic outdoors, complete with china and linens.

Members of the Elite Club, in the upper photograph, are identified from left to right: (front row) Cora Van Every Hillman, Flow Ripley Elliott, Georgia Marshall Phillips, Grace Campbell Bruce, and Harriett Van Schaik Patterson; (two in back of front row) Mrs. Lee and Bertha Benedict; (middle row) Marian Patterson, Winifred Stiff Paris, Susie Rix Pomeroy, Lina Britten Plumb, Mamie Ripley, and Bertha Patterson; (back row) Frannie Sexton Joslin, Susie Decou Buckoven, Etta Ostrander, Edith Allen, Addie Tenney McDonald, Veva Case, Grace Shepard, and Belle Baird Leeson.

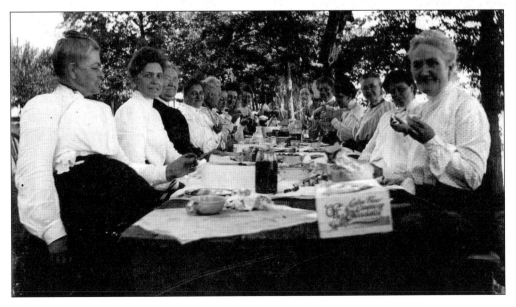

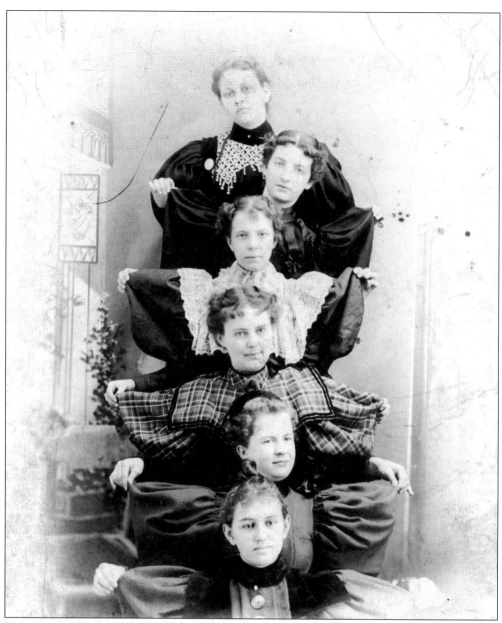

VICTORIAN LADIES' FASHIONS, C. 1895. Styles of women's clothing were constantly evolving, reflecting changes in culture, women's status, and new technology. In the late 1800s, the hoop skirts of the 1860s and the bustles of the 1870s and 1880s gave to a simple bell-shaped skirt. The bodices were fitted. The area of interest in the garment went to the sleeves, which became very full. The leg of mutton sleeve was wrist length, narrow at the bottom, and puffed at the top. On occasion this style was very exaggerated.

In a small community, people make friends early on in their childhood and keep those friends all their lives. These young ladies are in the photographer's studio showing off their newest dresses with leg of mutton sleeves. Pictured from top to bottom are Ethel Voorheis VanRiper, Elizabeth Arthur, Maude Church McGonegal, Emma Lamb Hadley, Tracey Botsford Arthur, and Gertrude Wright Alger.

FORMAL FRIENDS PORTRAIT. Pictured here are, from left to right: (front row) Gertrude Wright Alger, Ethel Voorheis VanRiper, and Tracey Botsford Arthur Brage; (back row) unidentified, Maude Church McGonegal, Emma Lamb Hadley, and Elizabeth Arthur.

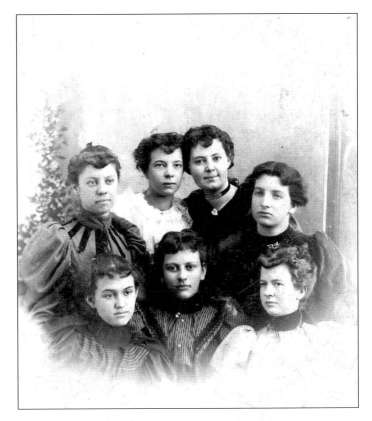

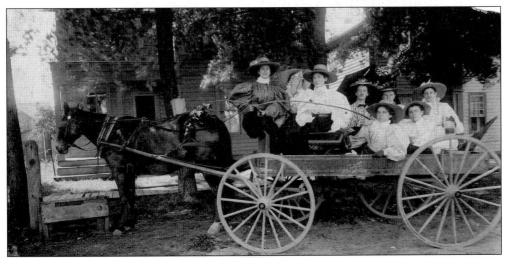

WOMEN ON WAGON. These ladies are all dressed up in their Sunday best, including fitted, high-collared blouses enhanced with leg of mutton sleeves. Their footwear would have been boots, with laces or buttons, above the ankle. Only the poorest people went outdoors without their gloves and hats. Victorians wore stiff, confining clothing, which required an erect posture.

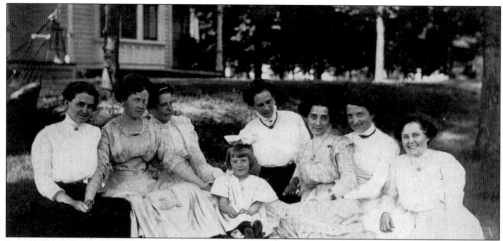

LAWN PARTY. Here are the ladies a few years later, after one of them has had a child, relaxing on the lawn. From left are Gertrude Wright Alger, Tracey Botsford Arthur, Maude Church McGonegal, Ethel Voorheis VanRiper, an unidentified child, Elizabeth Arthur, and Emma Lamb Hadley.

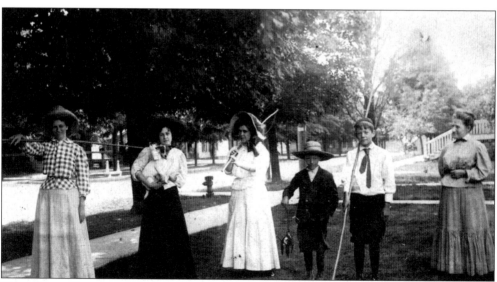

HAVE GONE FISHING. The people pictured above likely visited Stiff's Mill Pond, or one of the Shiawassee River tributaries, all within walking distance of Dr. Bussey's yard on South Saginaw Street. With their fishing poles and catch are, from left to right: Ethel Van Riper, Jenny Haddon, unidentified, Elliott Everett Van Riper, Dewitt, and Mrs. Van Riper.

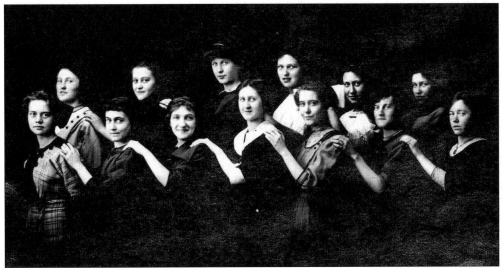

WOMEN OF 1915. Women's fashions have changed over the years, as evidenced by these photographs. Pictured from left are as follows: (front row) Phoebe Barrett, Hazel Slocum, Margaret McGinnis, Alice Fitzpatrick, Erma VanDensen, Evaline Frazer, and Vera Cook; (back row) Ruth Henning, unidentified—but calls herself "the real old lady of the group," Mabel Hotchkiss, Doric McDonald, Mildred Gundry, and Leora Downing.

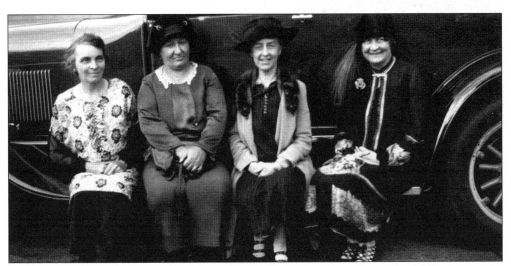

WOMEN ON CAR RUNNING BOARD, C. 1920. "Here we are in front of Ada's home on the running board of Macy's car." There is nothing like dressing up and going for a ride in a snappy new roadster. The women are sporting cloche hats and the shorter skirts of the 1920s era, along with heels for daywear.

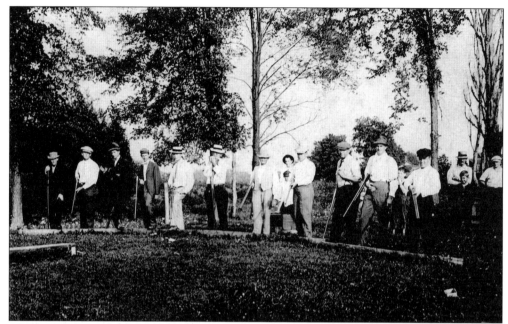

HOLLY GUN CLUB, SEPTEMBER 1, 1913. One of the local pastimes that was considered a sport was skeet shooting. During the Holly Centennial Celebration of 1938, the program listed an event held by the Skeet Shoot at the Holly Gun Club. The competition offered $65 in prizes.

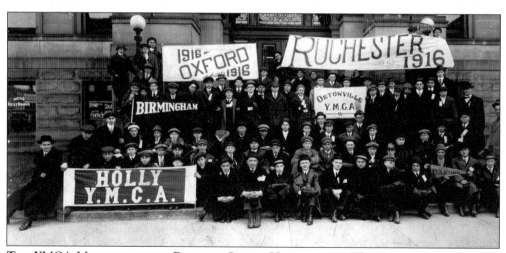

THE YMCA MEETING AT THE PONTIAC COURT HOUSE, 1916. The Young Men's Christian Association became important as a home away from home for many young men. A lot of the communities of Northwest Oakland County participated in this conference, including Birmingham, Holly, Ortonville, Oxford, and Rochester.

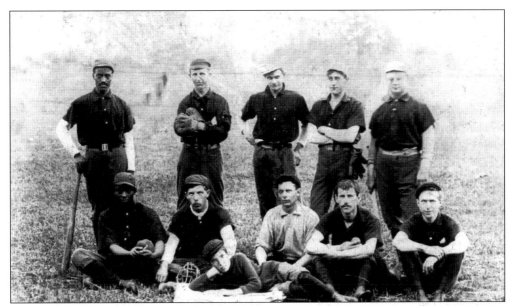

THE HOLLY BASEBALL NINE. This baseball team played at Rose Center on July 4, 1896. In the front row is "Tib" Joe Bensett. The other players are, from left: (middle row) Mr. Dunbar, Frank Bridgeman, Joe McGaffey, Dick Rheaum, and Ray Cornell; (back row) Elmer Dunbar, Clarence Hillman, Murray Bakham, Joe Covert, and Guy Harding.

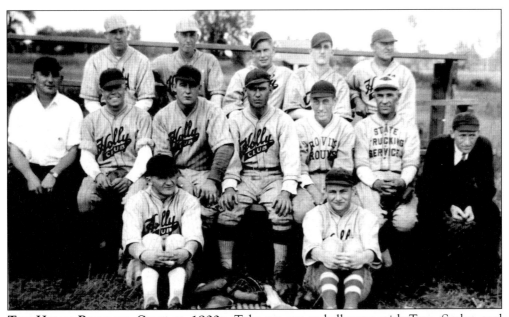

THE HOLLY BASEBALL CLUB, c. 1900s. Take me out to ball game with Tom, Seeley, and Herb. The men in the front row are all unidentified. The men in the middle row are all unidentified except Umpire Herman Schelp. In the back row, from the left are Tom Shine, Seeley Tinsman, and Herb Hartz, while the rest are also unidentified.

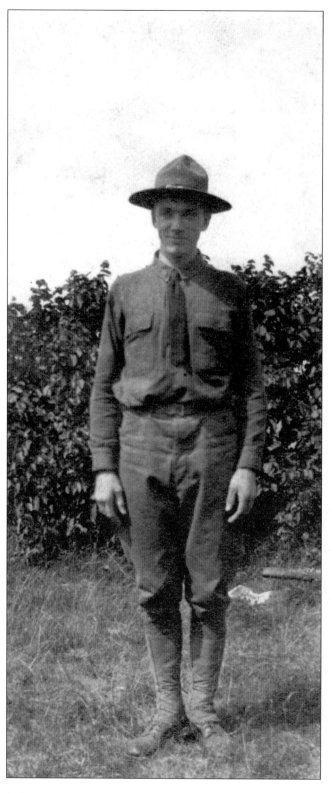

AMEL SCHWARTZ, WORLD WAR I. Amel was the first Holly boy to lose his life in World War I. He left the village on November 19, 1917. On July 19, his parents received word that he was wounded. It was believed that he recovered and went back to the front. Official notice came from General Pershing that he was killed in action in France on August 1, 1918. He was only 21 years of age. Memorial services were held on September 22, 1918, but it was not until July 19, 1922 that his body was returned for burial in Lakeside Cemetery. American Legion Post 149 was named in his honor.

On June 28, 1918, he sent a letter to his sister: "Dear Sister and all: I received your letter of May 9 on June 28, I was glad to hear from you. Well, the 12th was my birthday, [it was not] quite the same as [it was] last year. I caught a nice batch of fish then, but I am not fishing any now, will give them a chance to grow, so when I get back they will be bigger. I saw two airplanes come down in one day. They battle every day and I often watch them. Once in awhile, one is shot down. I saw one burn in the air, and it came down like a ton of bricks. Tobacco is scarce here."

ARTHUR SCHWARTZ, WORLD WAR I. Amel's letter continues with "I suppose you hear from Arthur and I wonder how John likes it at Camp Custer. He'll find out what I told him about last winter; it isn't all play. This leaves me in good health and I hope it finds you all the same. Must ring off now. Tell all the boys I said hello. Goodbye, you loving brother." Arthur Schwartz, Amel's brother, was stationed in the United States Air Corps, in Lonoke, Arkansas, and his other brother, John, also saw action in France. They both returned home safely.

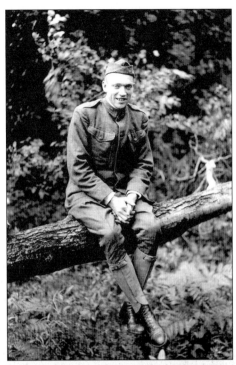

VETERANS HONORED IN FRONT OF HOLLY TOWNSHIP HALL. Veterans from the Civil War through World War I are honored here. Identified are, from left: (front row) J.P.W. Mothersill, Handy Austin, S.D. Mosher, and William Austin; (back row) W.F. Boening, H.O. Benson, E. Van Riper, F. Hooser, R.E. Addis, J. Perry, and Arthur Schwartz.

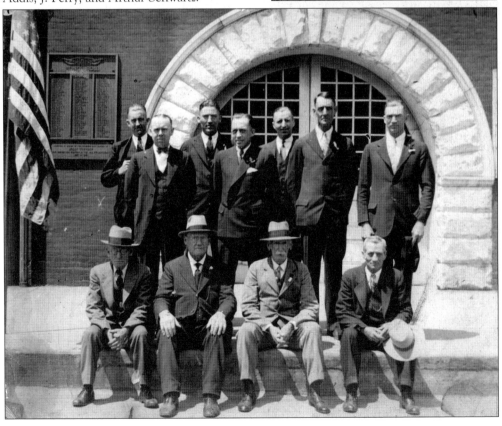

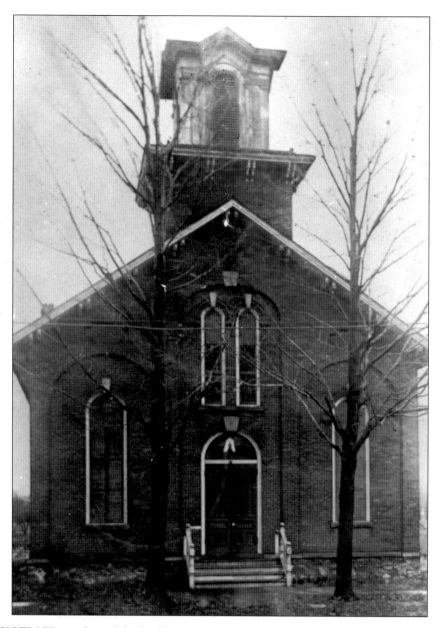

THE KOTM HALL. One of the buildings in constant use in the village once served a different purpose. The Reverend L. Wicker was responsible for building the church in 1854. Located on Washington Street, the structure was first used by the Maccabees. It was purchased by the Masonic Order in 1927, and is still in use today.

The 1938 centennial edition of the *Holly Herald* writes: "Masonry cannot advertise as secrecy is the very essence of its being. It is a brotherhood composed of symbolic Master, Fellow and Apprentices. . . . The strand of Masonry appears in every important event in American history, in the affairs in the State of Michigan and of the Township and Village of Holly."

The Order of the Eastern Star is a feminine counterpart of the Fraternal Organization of the Masons. Their ideals include caring for the sick, widows, and orphans, and providing educational scholarships. (Photo Courtesy Don Winglemire and Bob Harding.)

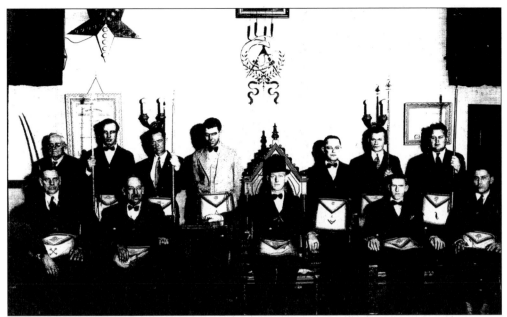

HOLLY LODGE, NUMBER 134, F.A.M. OFFICERS, 1933. The officers pictured here are, from left: Pat Gordon, Bob Allen, Walt Arnold, George Patterson, and unidentified; (back row) unidentified, unidentified, George Welch, unidentified, unidentified, Ferdinand Schultz, and unidentified. (Photo Courtesy of Bob Harding and Don Winglemire.)

HOLLY LODGE, 1927. On Friday evening, January 28, 1927, the Holly Lodge Masons held a special program to entertain the Austin Lodge from Davisburg, Michigan. They started the evening with a seafood meal. Promptly at 7:30 p.m., the curtain rose to a theatrical production. Act I, "Why Boys Leave Home," was assisted by the entire company. Act II brought "The Perils of a Large City," performed by a cast of highly trained experts. There followed an intermission of specialties that "must be seen to be appreciated." The Act III finale was "I Didn't Raise My Boy to Be a Soldier."

HOLLY LODGE, No. 134, F. & A. M.

CORDIALLY INVITES YOU TO BE PRESENT AT A

THIRD
DEGREE

Friday Evening, January 28th, A. D. 1927

ACT 1................Why Boys Leave Home................Assisted by the entire company

ACT 2................The Perils of a Large City............By a cast of highly trained experts

Specialties by Brothers Wendell, Seeley and Mott
(Must be seen to be appreciated)

ACT 3................I Didn't Raise My Boy to Be a Soldier................Profusely illustrated

AUSTIN LODGE, No. 48, DAVISBURG, MICHIGAN
WILL BE PRESENT

Sea-food, sinkers, etc., at 6:30 P. M.
Curtain rises at 7:30 P. M., sharp

MUSIC................By Grinnell (Horse-power by Brother Nelson)

SCENERY AND CEILING............By Mother Nature

LIGHTS................By Consumers

ROOF................By Brother Wendell (Positively no rain-checks issued)

ATMOSPHERE ....By Brother O. W. East

WARNING

Brothers who desire seats reserved in bomb-proof section, kindly make application to Brothers Tucker or Murray

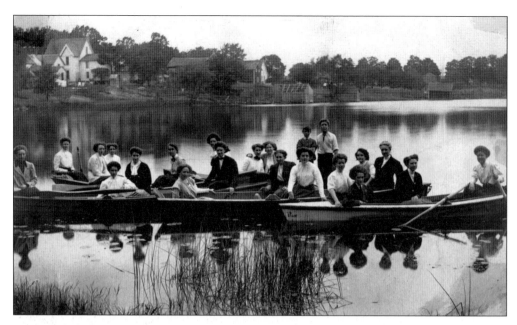

SIMONSON LAKE, 1909–1917. There were plenty of recreational opportunities in the community. A canal was hand dug out of the marshland between Simonson and Bush Lakes for a contract cost of $1,200. In 1889, Joe Winglemire bought a small steamboat whose whistle hailed families to board for a two-mile-long cruise. The round trip was 25¢ and 10¢ for children. The banker J.S. Simonson also had a steam launch on the water and the shoreline became dotted with canoes and rowboats. The two boats were called the *Star* and the *Myrtle D.*, which could carry as many as 75 people. Residents could spend a day in the park with music and dancing without leaving the limits of Holly; it was all within walking distance. Holly became recognized as a summer resort, and some of the cottages still exist.

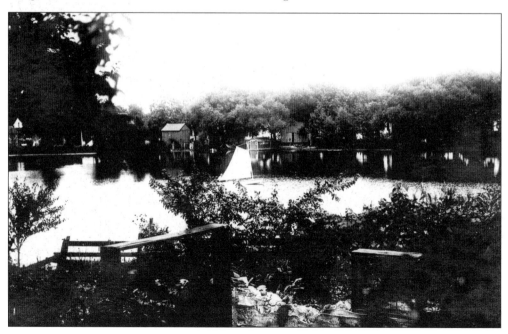

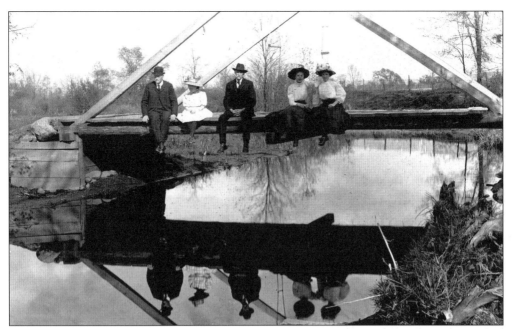

BRIDGE IN HOLLY, 1909. These people spent a quiet Sunday afternoon or evening enjoying the Shiawassee River after a stroll. They did not bring their fishing poles this time. (Photo Courtesy of Don Simons.)

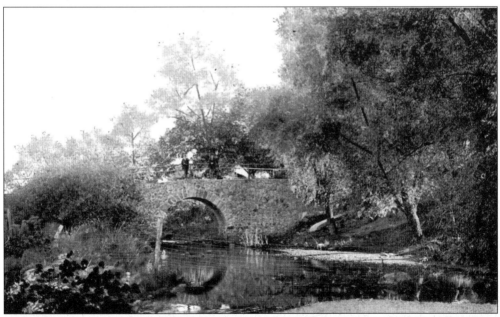

MORRISON STREET BRIDGE. The first bridge over the Shiawassee River, on Morrison Road, was built of logs and planks. It had no hand railing. The structure was replaced in 1906 by a stone arch bridge with iron pipe railing. This was before the road was paved. (Photo courtesy of Anthony Doran.)

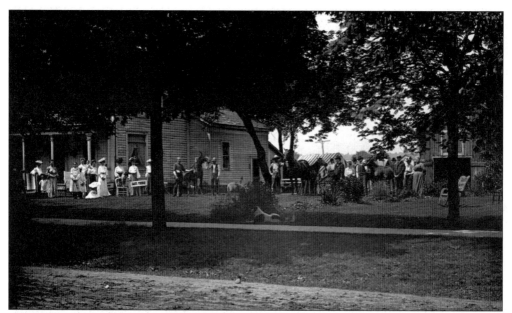

THE BUSSEY YARD, JULY 4, 1903 PICNIC. This is the view of the lawn and residence of E.D. Bussey on South Saginaw Street. Holidays usually meant a picnic get-together for family and friends. Some of the people attending included the John Lane Family, the Alger Family, Dr. Barthomew, the family dogs, Bill and Sport, and the young three-week-old colt, who frightened Seely Mosher out of the picture. In the distance the Jarvis Section, Spy-on-Kop, Skybow Hill, and the Baptist Hill Ridge are visible.

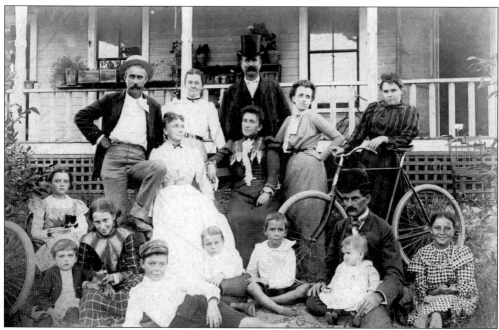

THE SEELEY FAMILY IN THEIR FRONT YARD. Mr. C.C. Seeley, shown with the top hat, was a very successful businessman in Holly. He owned a drug store, and, at one time or another, the Seeley Ice Houses on Simonson Lake and the Seeley Coal and Wood Yard.

124

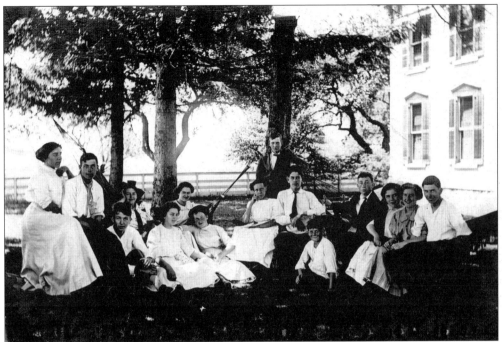

PICNIC AT THE HOME OF EUNICE DIVINE, 1912. These picnic-goers include, from left: (front row) Bert Jones, Hazel Waite, Marion Haddon, and George Cornell; (back row) Phoebe Divine, Arno Hulet, Daisy Hall, Verna Chaffee, Beatrice Henning, Kellon Mackey (standing), Paul Lockwood, Henry Seeley, Eunice Divine, Rotha Gibbs, and Emery Hulet.

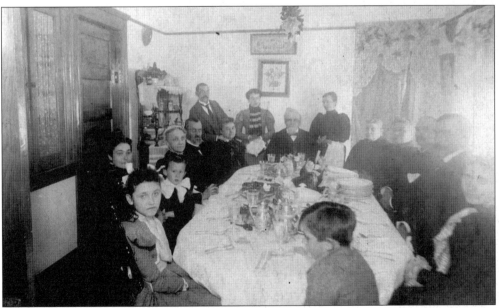

SUNDAY DINNER AT GRANDPA DOWNINGS'. One of the best Sunday traditions is dinner at a grandparent's house. The Moses Downings lived on a farm on East Holly Road in Holly Township. Moses and his brother, Henry, built an apple evaporator in Holly in 1877. They were both successful businessmen and eventually built houses in the village.

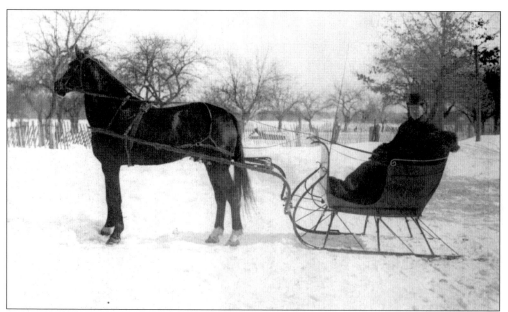

R. Day Patterson in Cutter. Robert Patterson surprised his aunt one morning when he rode his horse, Trixie, right up the stairs into her kitchen! He had the reputation for being a practical joker. Here he is with his horse and sleigh, otherwise known as a cutter. (Photo courtesy of Willa Mackie.)

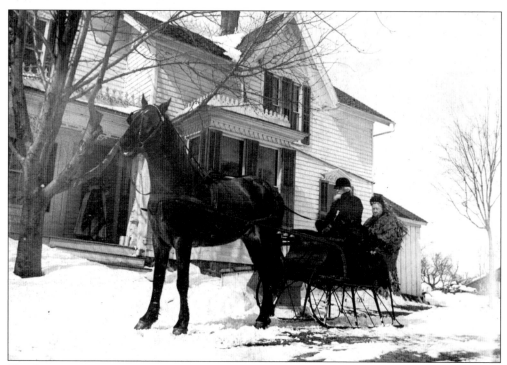

The Downings on Holly Road. This is Moses Downing driving a cutter on East Holly Road in Holly Township. This photograph was taken on the first of May, after a Michigan spring snowstorm at the farm. At a later time, the farm became the Smith Farm, which is there to this day.

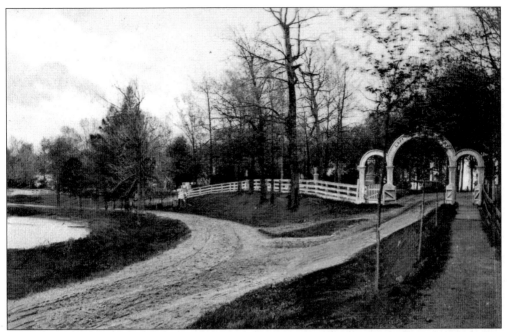

LAKESIDE CEMETERY, C. 1908. On the shores of Bush Lake, the oldest grave in Lakeside Cemetery dates back to 1841. There are also many Civil War gravesites. The largest monument is bronze and 25 feet tall. It was erected by Holly's Women's Relief Corps in honor of Holly, Rose, and Groveland Township soldiers between 1861 and 1865.

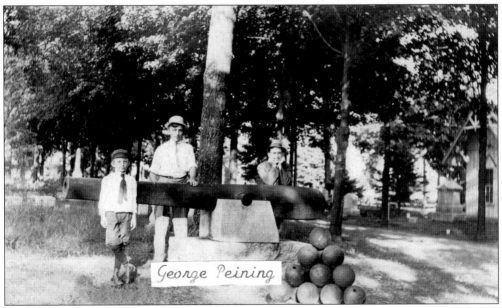

George Peining

CANNON AT THE LAKESIDE CEMETERY. One of the three cemeteries in the township, Lakeside has cannons as a Spanish American War Memorial. George Peining is pictured here, in the middle, with two unidentified friends.

127

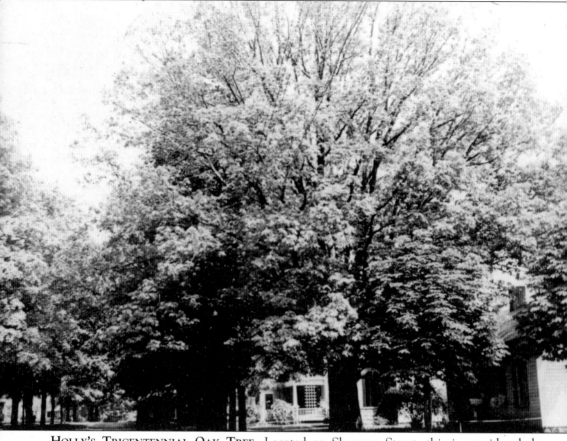

HOLLY'S TRICENTENNIAL OAK TREE. Located on Sherman Street, this is considered the biggest oak tree in the area, and the oldest. Some of the senior residents of the Village of Holly say that there has been little change in the tree since their childhood. It has withstood the advent of the white man in this locality and has a spread of over 80 feet. (Photo courtesy of Lisa Clark.)

Printed in Holly's Centennial Celebration Program from July of 1938, as part of the grand finale, is this poem:

> Today we look around and see
> A city proud where once was only woods
> And churchly spires and streets and shops
> Where once the Indian's lonely wigwams stood.
>
> Today we look with pride upon the work
> Started so long ago by stalwart men
> And gratitude more great than words
> Swells up within our hearts again.
>
> The yesterdays shall be most pleasantly recalled
> Todays shall soon be yesterdays, I ween,
> But the bright light which is tomorrow's sun,
> Shall be more brilliant than all the rest have been.